G000269712

CATHEDRALS IN THE SKY

Andrew Rajan

San Fernando Press

Copyright ©2014 Andrew Rajan

First Edition published 2014
by
San Fernando Press

This story is a work of fiction. Names, characters,
places and incidents are either products of the
author's imagination, or used fictitiously. Any
resemblance to actual events, locales or persons,
living or dead, is entirely coincidental. All rights
reserved

The moral right of the author has been asserted

Except for use in any review, no part of this
publication can be reproduced or transmitted in any
form, without prior permission in writing by Andrew
Rajan

ISBN 978-0-9930687-0-6

This book would not have been possible without the following people, all helping shape or inform it in some way; my deepest thanks to all of them. I hope in their estimation, it proved to be worth their while.

Barry Tomlinson -
Bedford Aeronautical Heritage Group
Pilot Roger 'Dodge' Bailey -
Shuttleworth Chief Pilot
Ian Larriman -
Shuttleworth Airframe Engineer
Steve McManus -
Shuttleworth Engineer, Engine Overhauls
Ivor Warne -
IWM Duxford

Roy Battersby, Georgie Black, Cherrie Burton, Melissa Centazzo, Deb Finlay, Anne O'Dowd, Jamie Sandford, Dr Helena Smith, and Victoria Worsley

Finally, the collections and intelligence at:
IWM Duxford
IWM Kennington
RAF Museum Hendon
The Shuttleworth Collection

Dedicated To The Very Few

Chapter I
2014

As no doubt countless parents had before me, I arrived on the first floor of St Mary's, Paddington A&E out of breath, highly distressed, a cold, wet patch gluing my shirt like guilt under the back of my jacket. Children's A&E Reception was manned by a neat topped, efficient lady in over-tight trousers, who was evidently well used to dealing with the exact profile I presented and, having ascertained my business there, she passed me a clip-file with a pen and a form to fill in pertaining to Tom, his details and my relation to him. Satisfied with my answers, she then handed me a badge, to be worn at all times and summonsed a nurse to chaperone me past the locked doors that led through to the Neuro Intensive Care Unit.

I took the opportunity to catch my breath and rub antiseptic alcohol over my sweaty palms, however doing so only served to make my clammy hands feel even worse. I knew Tom was alive, but that his condition was not yet considered stable. As we walked down corridors, the nurse, whose name had slipped me by completely, began explaining what I already knew: He had been cycling home from school and collided with a stationary car.

Typical Tom. Head down, pedalling like Fury, oblivious to the world around him. It had taken a month of reverse psychology, badgering and dire threats to get him to dispense with his iPod when cycling, but there was absolutely nothing I could do about his attention. He had pedalled full pelt into a parked car and shot over the handlebars, smashing his face on the bonnet, finally being caught by a passing car as he bounced off. The driver had fortunately stopped, as had a young witness walking her neighbour's dog and it was she who called an ambulance to the scene.

Tom had managed to powder his two front teeth, crack his jaw and his nose. He also had bruised ribs, a broken collarbone and a broken leg.

"He was unconscious upon arrival and the CT scan showed a subdural haematoma. He was taken into theatre straight away for decompression of the brain. He's now sedated, on a ventilator..." The nurse was softly spoken in a pleasant, careful, business-like manner I took to. We rounded the last corner and I faltered at what was obviously the end of his curtained bed.

I wasn't sure if I was prepared to see him and not flinch or cry. Being unconscious, I felt a pulse of guilt as I realised I was glad he wouldn't be able to perceive me reacting to his sad, broken self. The nurse made a gap and ushered me in. I braced, but there wasn't a lot to see of my boy. He was under a tent in the bed, his right arm in a supported sling and his face so bandaged he was completely obscured, aside from a small, unruly tuft of black hair that had escaped the clutches of the mummification.

Even on a standard ward, he was plugged into an array of machines, most of which I could have had an educated guess as to their purpose. I stood looking at the picture he made, so different from the last one I recalled, as he'd set off that morning. But my alarm levels subsided a little, just by standing there, looking at him. I wanted to hold him, but was afraid even to touch, for fear of dislodging some paraphernalia or causing hurt. I contented myself with putting a hand softly on the end of the bed.

I looked to the nurse, not sure what was expected of me. Busy with her checks, she indicated a chair on the other side that I was free to use and offered 'a restaurant on the ground floor near to the main entrance', or 'vending machines by the lifts', if I was at all hungry. I 'could stay as long as I wanted' and 'he could, in all likelihood, hear me'. With a sympathetic smile, she made a last check on Tom's position and, sweeping the curtain shut behind her, left me to my own devices. After a few moments looking at my boy as I calibrated my nascent situation, I took off my jacket and dumped my bag gratefully on the floor. There was a small flat-screen TV on an adjustable arm over the end of Tom's bed. I had no intention of employing it, but realised it was a pay TV that required a credit card to use. How things had changed.

This said, overall, I was very impressed with the facilities, cleanliness, care and attention that I had observed. Years of watching the news and countless documentaries about hospitals- privatisation, mismanagement, people dying of dehydration, murderous nurses and MRSA, my inner notion of what hospitals were had, I realised, diminished to the point that I expected to be ignored, my child mistreated and all in filthy conditions administered by surly staff. It had been a while since I'd been inside a hospital.

Tom slept on. Aware I should perhaps be communicating with him, I leant in, but could think of absolutely nothing to say. I couldn't admonish him, talk about the weather, or my day at work; all were redundant, ridiculous under the circumstances. Looking across him, the various digital waves appeared reassuringly uniform, although I had no idea if they were uniformly good, exactly. Words absent, I leant back in my chair for the first time and suddenly realised how shattered I was, the sweat on my shirt making its presence known. Without looking, I knew I had neither a book nor sustenance in my bag. I resolved to leave both bag and coat and find a toilet at least, whilst I considered my next move.

Clarity returned with each passing second that I emptied my bladder and I then delighted in the opportunity to wash my hands the traditional way, with those elbow taps, peculiar to medical establishments. Again I was struck by how spotless the facilities were. As I attempted to straighten my crumpled linen shirt, pushing my hair into something resembling presentable, I remembered I should text Bridget. There was no wife to ring, or parents to reassure. Tom and I essentially had only each other. But, as my closest friend, Bridget would be waiting for my call.

I hung around the loo as I waited for the connection. I liked to walk as I talked, for some reason. It made the words flow easier and doing this in an empty corridor felt less intrusive than chatting sotto voce on the ward. My stomach growled at me rebelliously and I eyed a vending machine as I circled erratically, completing the litany of injuries my boy had sustained whilst playing car billiards. I had imagined the first impact and thanked my stars that he had at least hit the car front on. If he had hit the backend, there was a high chance he could have met with a rear windscreen, rather than a flat bonnet. I wondered what make it was.

Bridget was more concerned that I didn't forget to take care of myself, as it seemed there was little else to do for Tom at the present time. She was right of course. My body had been telling me much the same for a few hours.

As I returned to my ward however, it was still the make and model of the parked car that occupied my thoughts. If it was at all modern-built, it would have had plastic bumpers and may have actually sustained significant damage, considering the speed he would have been travelling. Not sure what I was looking for, I rooted through his backpack, then wondered what had become of his bike. Nothing appeared to be missing from his bag, even his watch and wallet were there, sealed in a plastic hospital bag. I looked down at him. He remained resolutely unchanged, his breathing slow and steady, he was completely unmoved from the position I had first seen him in, giving me the sense it was going to be a long vigil. I told His Inertness I was taking charge of his valuables and stuffed them into my already overstuffed bag.

I wondered at the different childhoods he and I experienced. Mine revolved around my mother and his around me. My whole parenthood bent on making sure the shortfalls in my own upbringing were not repeated with him. At his age, I quite liked hospitals.

I'd grown up in the Seventies. Well, the Sixties and Seventies. By the time I was Tom's age, it was the mid-Seventies. He was a good kid. Really, I'd been blessed. At the age of 12, his greatest transgression was to not be paying attention. At his age, I suppose I was a real tearaway. Not in a boisterous, beating people up, shouty kind of way, but a quiet, fire-starter one. I had taken to pilfering school supplies of meths and turps; I decanted them into glass phials in the science lab and secreted them out in my satchel. On the way home, I would stop in the playing field to hunt for mushrooms growing wild; in the days of innocence, before magic mushrooms or the notion of DDT were even on the map. They were always to be found in the darkest, lushest rings of grass, as if either they were good for grass growth, or they only grew where the soil was best. I favoured the former though, as the grass was only lush in the mushroom ring, not in any irregular pattern. Then I would pass by a building site.

We lived on the edge of aggressive housing development. As children, building sites, like parks, fields, woods, allotments and backstreets were legitimate playgrounds, in the days when you went out to play in the afternoon and new house builds weren't fenced off. The local kids would gather on opposing bulldozed earth mounds and throw rock hard, sun-baked lumps of mud at each other. It was war, fought with the ferocity and commitment that kids have.

In hindsight, I was lucky never to have been struck by one, because it was literally no different to being stoned. I also had a fierce and accurate throwing arm. When left alone however, on my dawdles home, these same sites could also be a natural draw to any budding pyromaniac. The heady stink of pink paraffin coming from the portable cement mixers and all the straw used as packing for the stacks of flushed, ugly LBC bricks.

Methylated spirits and turpentine don't mix. When poured into a glass bottle, they separate out, one purple, one clear, a deliciously thick meniscus soon reappearing between the two, however much you shook the bottle. To a ten year old, that sat squarely on the side of magical. Then, all one needed to do was pull out a few bricks from the stack, gather the straw to create a nest for the bottle and a line to the fuel patch underpinning the mixer, unscrew the fuel cap, use a match to coax the impromptu fuse into life and then peg it before the acrid straw made too much of a smoking betrayal. If you got it right, you could destroy an entire stack of bricks, whilst dispatching a cement mixer to boot.

Looking back on it now, I realise my beef was with the destruction of the wilderness that had existed before, as much as the hit from the doing of it. The march of progress wiped out the orchards, the fields and allotments, the natural wilderness I much preferred to lose myself in, but it really is no defence for arson. Come to think of it, I'd set light to an orchard before too, albeit by mistake, when I chose to set fire to a wasps nest in the middle of a summer holiday heat wave. I was never caught for any of these many transgressions, 'Lord knows how, but I must have contributed significantly to the modern practice of ring-fencing building sites, alarms, security patrols and CCTV.

Mothers have a sixth sense about these things. It was more the silent insolence that did for her, although she must also have wondered about the half-used packs of matches found in my shorts too, on occasion. She was a single parent trying to hold down a full-time, poorly paid job, feed me and put me through school.

I was a constant drain on all resources, an ingrate even, but then, I was also only a minor. I didn't understand the sacrifice a parent undertakes when they commit to raising a child to the best of their abilities. Tom, from time to time, would ask me about my childhood and I would always deflect. It was easy, in the moment, to move him on to another topic, but he had also got to an age now where he was aware I was doing it. I needed to tell him more. I just didn't know how to, without plunging into the pain of it all. Or admitting to grand arson.

My mother had incandescent rages. This meant that even when she wasn't angry, every moment of every day had this Damocles possibility hanging over it, whether it was misbehaving at school, forgetting something, or putting a foot out of place at home. One particular occasion, I had taken a Pyrex bowl in to school for Home Economics, as we were to be cooking apple crumble. It sat in a plastic bag on my table and as I lifted the lid to get to my exercise books, I took a firm hold of the bag to prevent mishap, however, I had only the bottom of the bag. As I lifted my table top up, the bowl slid out of the bag and smashed into a million smithereens on the floor.

I'll never forget the paralysing sense of dread that gripped my entire body. I sat there, looking at all the tiny, un-mendable shards skating far and wide under table and chair and all I could think of was the beating I was going to get when I got home. My teacher was very sweet. I don't think she could understand the impact the accident had on me. To her, it was a broken bowl- unfortunate, but no more than that. I cannot remember anything else that day. I don't even know whether I cleared up the mess or someone else did; I was in a state of shock. In the last class of the day, without a bowl to put it all in, I didn't get to make the pudding and was sent back home with all my ingredients.

When I got back, as expected, I had my ears boxed at the front door and, during dinner was kicked sharply in the shins, under the table. She made an apple crumble, but I wasn't allowed any. Later that night on my way early to bed, she picked me up and threw me downstairs. As I curled up sobbing, I felt a dampness on my pillow that wasn't just tears. Switching the light on, I discovered I was bleeding from one ear. It took a while before I mustered the courage to go back and show her what had happened, as I knew my bleeding was yet another inconvenience and also entirely my own fault. I may even get another beating for bleeding all over the bed linen. In the end however, I did so. Someone needed to tell her to stop.

By the time we arrived at A&E and I was hyperventilating, so was made to breath into a paper-bag, as she explained to the friendly nurse that I had 'fallen downstairs'. The damage proved minor though and shortly thereafter, I was discharged and we travelled back home in silence.

I resolved there and then that I would tell Tom more of the story of my childhood, albeit in judiciously censored fashion. He knew of my first love and I had introduced him to poetry at a very young age, but there really was no need for him to know I was a very successful, enthusiastic young pyromaniac; although revisiting the Spitfire was something he'd never bored of, however many times in the telling, he still deserved to know more... to know other. But I still wanted to avoid tales of terror and that was all my early childhood consisted of: different degrees of terror.

The inbuilt guilt and hazard of being a single parent, as with my own mother, was karmically evident to me now and I offered up a small prayer in her remembrance as, having paused again for the sliding door, Shifting in my seat, I peered over him, careful not to breathe excessively, I reflected that our lives mirrored each other in that one miserable fact; we had both lost our mothers far too soon. In my case, twice.

Chapter II
1976

Ash came to us when he was twelve. Laura and I had just two short conversations over dinner and the decision was made. Our daughter had more than enough on her plate and taking him out of the equation would demonstrably help, so there really was nothing more to be discussed. Having said which, the wife was more nervous than I was about it.

He was a jacknife of a lad: sharp, dark urban eyes that took you in and turned you over in a glance, like some Fifties fence passing seasoned fingers over stolen silver, ones perceived worth seemed summed up in seconds. I wasn't at all sure if I trusted him, in fact, if I'm honest, I knew I didn't. But I also reasoned that he'd missed out on a lot, growing up in town, without a Dad.

It would be a seismic change, but perhaps one that would be good for him. Laura's concerns weren't so much that she didn't trust him; she had such an open heart when it came to people. No, it was more regarding the fact that he was brown and Kent so very white. She worried that he wouldn't fit in, would get singled out and picked on.

I assured her that 'life now' was very different from 'life then' and that 'he would make his way'. I might have added that I wasn't at all certain that this was true, but that with his street-wise sensibilities, I felt sure he would indeed 'make his way', regardless of who might be trampled en route. Besides, he would have the whole farm to 'find' himself in.

Collecting Ash from the station, I tried to imagine what shape he'd be in. It's quite something to leave home, leave your mother and move in with people you don't know well, even if they are family. But then, whether or not he had any conscious memory of it, he'd done it all before.

He appeared on cue as the train pulled out, a subdued figure ambling over the bridge under ascendant sun, already hot, carrying only two bags, some flowers crushed in his armpit for Laura, pushing through the cloud of insects that plagued his path. After making a little misjudged small talk about school, from which I'd temporarily forgotten he'd been expelled, I left him free to paddle about in his own thoughts as he watched the world pass by the car window. We travelled in this not uneasy silence for the rest of the trip, punctuated only by the insistent squeak of windscreen wipers, as I attempted to clear the morass of ladybirds and dust from the windscreen with a substandard blade I needed to replace and an insufficient squirt of water.

Swallowtail Farm was hidden by a nondescript entrance to a narrow, winding driveway on a fast stretch of road, such that unless you knew it was there, you might pass right by. A small power substation also shared the top of the drive, with one of those ubiquitous, solid, high wooden fences, enclosing a battleship grey metal lump, with power cables dipping in from the back; categorical 'Danger of Death' and 'High Voltage' signs plastered on every side. On top sat an Early Warning siren. Passing that, the drive quickly got even narrower between low fruit trees and cindered black, as opposed to tarmac, eventually opening out into a courtyard, stables on the right, with their own concrete courtyard and the farmhouse on the left.

Many of the stables had been converted into alternative plots and a fledgling, if mostly absent electronics company rented space there, but there were still a couple of operational stables hired out to locals, giving home to horses in absence of their own facilities. A converted barn directly annexed the farmhouse with another traditional hay-barn on the end of it, a pigpen out front. There was yet another whole, separate converted barn building containing my substantial workshop. Beyond that, the land sloped gently down and right towards the henhouse, the two top fields and then three bottom fields that ended at the start of a stretch of common woodland. From the house, apart from the sections occluded by the barns, one could get a good South Easterly view, not only of the land belonging to the farm, but also the woods beyond Baggett's Pond and the rolling Kent countryside beyond.

Hamlet came bounding out and Laura made a fuss of Ash as soon as we exited the car. An excitable Great Dane, Hamlet was well over six feet tall when up on his hind legs and quite a proposition if you weren't expecting forepaws on each shoulder and an enthusiastic slathering across the chops. Laura had baked a cake and, with the bread also rising in the oven, the house smelled even more warm and welcoming than usual.

Not fully thinking it through, I'd agreed not to house him in the guest room, Laura utilising his impending arrival as an excuse to clear out one of the unused bedrooms of the 'clutter' she felt threatened to 'overwhelm the house'. It was true; I liked storing useful things. I had two barns and an outhouse full of stuff, but she rather drew the line at the front doorstep of the farmhouse and it was a constant bone of contention how many of the rooms of the house were now, as she put it, 'out of commission'. They were being put to excellent use, as far as I could see. It wasn't as if we were going to have any more children after all, was it? Well, not until now.

So, I cleared the nice-sized room above the kitchen; a sunny aspect, with a lovely view over the yard, the far fence and out across the patchwork rolling woods and fields. Laura washed the curtains and made it all cosy, as women do. It did surprise me that it took a full week to clear as, once I managed to reach them, I also had to empty the wardrobe and a large chest of drawers. Laura lined up bin bags, cheekily offering to order a skip, in the hope I wouldn't simply shuffle and relocate items, but actually be rid of some. If she was disappointed, it didn't show. As surmised, she was more than pleased with the 'reclamation' of a room in the house.

Almost the first thing Ash did upon entering his new bedroom was to climb on a chair and hang an *Airfix* Spitfire from the ceiling. Closing the door behind me, I left him to it.

He sat around for the first couple of days, then wandered listlessly about the farm in a manner reflecting the still, stifling weather, seemingly content not to get drawn into anything much at all. He needed no introduction to Hamlet, the ducks, the pigs Pinky and Perky, or the chickens, but Laura coaxed him gently into doing a few jobs around the place; general feeding, collecting the eggs, and sporadically refilling the duck pond, but I was never comfortable with the concept of coercing him into some sort of Home Help.

We did have quiet discussions periodically over this time, Laura concerned that we give him 'something useful to do to take his mind off things', as she would have it. I introduced him to Russ, the sometime help around the farm, but at 15 and a taciturn country boy through and through, the pair of them really had very little in common, plus a seemingly implacable unwillingness to even find out.

We didn't have a television, the nearest useful shop was 30minutes away and there wasn't a bicycle on the farm small enough for him to reach the pedals. It could all go either way.

Chapter III
   1941

'Is ironical, but it was Germany's early success
t'ru Lufthansa flying to Bermuda dat first capture'
my imagination. Previous' to dat, I never consider
flying serious' before dat, but took to aviation with de
sole intention of applyin' to Lufthansa for a job 'pon
graduatin', wantin' to spread my wings not in de US,
but all the way over Europe side.

   I was fortunate to have a farder enthusiastic to
have me succeed, even though it would eventually tek
me away from him and, despite me mudder'
protestation', he encourage me movin' to Caracas to
get me wing'.

   But de many weeks of trainin' pluck open my
eyes, changin' me perspective. Without dem love an'
support, I could now see de benefit to stayin' closer
to home, so when de opportunity come up to fly
instead for de world leaders, for Pan Am, from
Nassau through Port o' Spain and over Mexico City
and Buenos Aires, I took it, wid the excuse that me
mudder would miss me too much, when- de truth? I
woulda miss' both of them more, ma's goat roti bein'
a good case in point. No one mek bread like me
mudder.

   Just t'ree years later, I find myself alone in
Allahabad, India, my firs' time der, clutching me
farder's ashes, to empty dem into de Ganges, as he
would want. He always want' to go visit de
homeland, meet distant cousin, but most of all, for de
great Kumbh Mela. But heart disease took him before
he make it over.

   As de dawn broke on the soft ripple, de oarsman
waitin' patiently silent behind, I offer prayer to Shiva,

lean over de side o' de skiff, and pour him ashes and
marigold at tha confluence of dem two great rivers.
Gust of wind blew dis fine dust of ash up back of me
arm -like a caress; like a final 'thank you' for bringin'
him home to res', one hundred year after him
ancestors left for Trinidad under the British, none of
them ever to return.

During the Mela it is said that at de dawn after de
full moon, at dat most Holy moment of change, a
space opens up between two world; de real and de
celestial, dis world and the spiritual, made holier by
the naked, ash-coated Sadhu's, dancing to music all
de way downg to de water's edge where dem bathe in
de early light, celebratin' de drop of nectar that fell
from the heavens into de river at dis exact point, at
the confluence o' de two river. De Sadhu's ash
signifyin' de death an' rebirth of life's everlastin'
cycle. I watching him ashes perish, futile tears stop'
in they pursuit by de surface swirl of de holy river.

Slow t'ree-day train journey back to de hot chaos,
de cows of Bombay and den finally aboard de packet
ship for Southampton, glad for some fresh sea air. So,
five days into dis trip when, on September four,
nineteen hundred an' t'irty nine, I learn of Britain's
Declaration of War against de German t'reat. Now,
my original plan had been a lickle train trip up to
London town, a lickle sightseein' and den Greenock
for de final boat home. But now, with dis momentous
news shocking de entire ship into some sombre
silence for what now awaited us all, I come up wid a
loose plan.

De war was no shock to us Trinis. We was
limin'… it had been discuss' at great length,

especially amongst us fraternity o' pilots. All of us felt a great bond, a fervent patriotism, a sympathy for de mudder country, England. If she wuz going to war, then there was never any doubt in my mind dat we would too, by hook or by crook. Most 'our discussion was how; whether it be t'rough de States, although there was some chattin' as to whether she would join de fray at all, which many of us doubted, or Cyanada. I favoured Cyanada. Only a few of us thought to go direct to Hengland.

But here I was. War declare' and on my way already. 'Seem Destiny. And beside, I couldna see how my original plan would even exist by the time I land, a ship home to Trinidad da first ting cancel' in a state of National Emergency.

By de time me board the 10.37 to Waterloo, me mind was made up; I would stroll to de RAF offices in London and offer my service to de King. I always wanting to fly Europe.

I duly present myself as fit an' able, a pilot wid a great deal of experience under me belt, but was soon strip' down o' de idea that I would be welcome wid open arm'. I was taken, yes, but not to fly, but to work as ground crew. I was post' to Lincolnshire, a cold, wet, flat, fog-bound place I had never heard of, on a base larger than anything I had ever experience previous', call' RAF Waddington, home to de Handley Page Hampden bomber.

It was the loneliest period of my life I can remember. No sense of camaraderie, I was definitely on de outside, although some much-needed warmth was afforded by Anne, de barmaid in de local tavern, albeit on de quiet, for fear of reparations from jealous airmen, or de local', for dat matter. I was pretty sure I wasn't her only, but I don' care. Even de food was grey. What I wouln' give for a fresh mango off de bush. For to suck de seeds of a cocoa pod dry.

T'ru this time, I write home as often as I can. I missin' me farder so much and feelin' for me mudder in dis time, wishin I could be der for her. Wishin' I could talk wid her, but felt it a bad idea to disavow me mudder of her ideals about Britain. From de day she born, she never set foot in anudder country, not even Venezuela. 'Woulda been pure selfish of me to have her worry on my behalf, when there was nuttin' to be done. And she write back advising me to integrate and how proud I mek her feel and de whole community inspired by me. But it don' matter how hard I try integratin', whatever small inroad I make on de one to one, they soon undone when de group got larger than two.

Tings change markedly though, as de war develop'. Once de Axis powers invade de low countries, everyting move up a gear. Bomber losses, especially de ol' Hampden, de Hereford, de poor Manchester and even de Wellington were fierce; but nuttin' was said. As ground crew it pay to keep your head down an' get on wid de job, but der were no denying de numbers that fail' to return.

There were moves to train up more an' more aircrew; I sense perhaps my day on de ground may be numbered, although I wasn't in love wid de idea of flyin' bomber, I cyan't refuse if it offered me. After all, why was I here in de first place?

De invite come unexpected, after lunch. I hurry over to de admin building, taking great care to wipe me feet as I step' indoor, me overalls less than crisp. What met me had me stun'. Having confirm' again

me flyin' credential, I was offer' a post not wid
bombers, but to learn wid fighter squadron. My salute
was so sharp, I almost pull a muscle! De immediate
ting I want to do was write me mudder an' tell her,
but firs' I need to get pack' and on de train south.
Mebe was my imagination, but in Englan', I always
feel warmer south.

Me mudder right though. Integration was de
answer. She may not be de mos' travel', but she wise.
One ting I find when I went to Caracas was dat I
quick move to soun' like de local. I tink it jus' an
effort for to fit in, is all. Us of the Indian Diaspora,
dat is what we famous for, fittin' in. When I was
youth, I had a English teacher, Miss Larkin. Lord!
Verry proper she was too. I study English fo' my first
degree. With not too much trouble, I could fit in; I
could lose my accent. I could lose the musical lilt
Anne was so fond of, in this crusty land that didn't
know how to dance, yes... If dat was what it cos'… if
that was what it *cost*, then that is what I would do.
Eat, sleep, drink, England. I would show them I could
be as English as the English. More so. There was a
language, a turn of phrase, a way of walking, of
holding one's cigarette. It wouldn't be hard. I
decided, before I even reached Northolt, to start a
training of my own, to become the man we used to
love to hate as a youth. By the time I hopped off the
ride to the base, there would be no trace of the boy
off the banana boat.

My apprenticeship didn't last long. Once they saw
me behind the stick of a Majister, I was soon moved
up to a Hurricane and then promoted to Flight
Sergeant to teach others. The gloves had come off
and fighting had started in earnest. There was a

distinct shortage of pilots, especially of the calibre needed to fly Hurricanes and Spitfires. Letters from home informed me of Trinidad's efforts to raise money for the war effort and buy planes for the front. And not only that, even Carib pilots were beginning to trickle through too. The call up seemed inevitable.

There appeared two distinct pilots' philosophies, every time one sank blindly into the snug, unyielding seat to be strapped down. Either that it would never happen to you, or this time was in all likelihood your last hour breathing canned air on God's Earth. One was then either reconciled with the latter, in the knowledge that one was doing one's level best and that many who had gone before were undoubtedly better men, or at least, better pilots, or one simply didn't want to die, period. This last option was the worst one to choose, for it was within this chink that fear could spread its wings inside the captive, even as he took flight.

The time I'd spent seconded to 303 Squadron, Northolt, up to the end of the so-called Battle of Britain had been trying. I just wanted combat, but was kept out of the front line, despite best efforts. I needed to be twice as good, twice as sharp as the man standing next to me. And patient. Ostensibly there to teach the Polish how to fly, we were all taught a lesson by those remarkable men, battle hardened on the German anvil above Poland, on how best to deal with the Flying Fritz. For these were fearless, dogged, astonishing pilots who, when eventually permitted by the RAF, took their Hurricanes into war with a gusto and a passion hammered from hatred, so creating a monumental hit rate, far surpassing any other

Squadron in the RAF, or the Luftwaffe, for that matter.

As a Flight Sergeant employed to take boys and ensure they didn't die from their own inexperience, arrogance or stupidity, I had perhaps grown a little blasé myself. Life soon travelled either at zero or 400mph, with very little inbetween. But I found my unexpected sense of kinship with these extraordinary men a surprise principally in its strength.

I understood all too fully their frustration with the stuffy hierarchy, the overpowering sense of being the mistrusted outsider, me the son of a Trini fisherman. After all, however adept we felt we might be, neither of us felt we belonged here, albeit for very different reasons.

As I limped home from France, skimming channel waves at less than 200 feet, port wing sporting an unseemly hole, weapons spent and no sign of a friendly aircraft in sight, reflecting on all the circumstances that had got me to this point, it was to these few that I drew for comfort; for example.

We were airborne at dawn, accompanying a bombing raid over Amiens. Flying at Angels 10 in a Shrew; a MkIIb Supermarine Spitfire. The trip out had been uneventful, despite an unfamiliar queasiness tagging some corner of my gut the moment I'd been woken.

Staggering blearily to the washstand and filling the bowl to shave, I waited for my eyes to focus properly by foaming some soap, eventually regarding my visage somewhat uneasily in the mirror, razor poised, a little afraid of what I might find. It was then that I stopped what I was doing and looked properly at the pasty brown man looking back, face half lathered in a thin foam, hair in disarray. Something I had avoided doing for the best part of a week. Certainly a lack of sun, but I looked old. As old as my old Dad, the last time I saw him alive. It was the same face, to all intents and purposes, the exact same face, but…

I hadn't previously considered myself the type to go into the air believing it would be my last hurrah. As tutor, I had got used to my charges being sent hither and yon across the land, pitched at whatever level their talent dictated, be it ground-crew, navigation, bombers or, if they were up to snuff, fighters.

But this war changed you, punished you on every level and, with whatever tenuous friendships you had on the line, to the point where you didn't know if anyone would still be there when you finally slumped into your favourite armchair (at the opposite end of the room from the Officers), in the end, you realised you only had yourself.

There were no conversations you could have with your family, your wife, your beau. Very rarely, with a look, you might catch someone and, in that split second, understand that other pilots understood. Only they. And then you realised in that same moment, that there was nothing that could be said to them either. And so you didn't. Most no doubt took that thought and pulled it back inside, dragged it deep, burying it in something soft, black and enveloping. Out of sight.

For myself, I resorted to the makings of a private diary. I wasn't sure how much really I should be documenting things, the recently revised Official Secrets Act being what it was, but I felt an even stronger compulsion to exorcise it somehow and if I wasn't to talk about it then, for the sake of my own sanity, I was going to write it down, even if I only ended up burning the blasted papers afterwards.

I always referred to my Spitfire as a 'Shrew'. I thought it apt when I was teaching young men, who quickly found out how unforgiving the Spitfire could be, the first time they were given the honour of taking one up. Many had trained in biplanes, in Majisters, even in Hurricanes, but nothing equipped them for their first time in a Shrew; all Shire horses... mules, against this thoroughbred, fire-spitting steed.

It appealed to my sense of the ridiculous that this peerless aircraft, a quantum leap from anything that had gone before, be named initially the Shrew. However, as I had gotten to know her and watched others falter in their attempts to control her, I felt the name oddly apposite. There was no taming her, but do it her way and she would do everything she was bid and more. Once you had a feel for her, there was nothing else to fly. She was the fleetest, most nimble, most beautiful, utterly responsive aircraft in the skies and for those of us that could, to a man, we knew we were all privileged to be there.

It was almost relief with which you scampered to that aircraft; the call to scramble a raison d'etre. It broke the tension of the waiting, made sense of the day. Made one feel one was actively doing something, giving it back to the Hun. 'Somewhere to funnel all the pent up energy, uncoil the spring.

But it was the oddest thing. At the very same time that you were rejoicing in the action, racing across the airfield as your ground crew fired her up, helping you into your parachute, leaping up the side, onto the wing and down into the cockpit relinquished just moments before by the airman now tightening your straps. A quick check of the instruments, a moments pause for the temperature to get up enough to move off and then the taxi to take off, all the time your roving eye pulled back to the temperature. She would overheat so fast on the ground; like a beached turtle baking in its own shell, so ungainly on land. But at that very same time, with so many things to think about, a thin slice of your mind wondered whether this would be your last scramble, your final call to arms.

Temperature rising, you refocus, concerned she would bounce about and damage a wingtip, the wheels being so close together. Unable to see anything over the imposing snout, you'd weave along, forever peering out sideways for a point of reference... too much throttle and you ended up on your nose, so front loaded, the massive Merlin III roaring, belching impatiently in front of you. With the puny air intake currently baffled by the wheels and travelling too slowly to help, even a couple of minutes inactivity on the ground with that monstrous powerhouse threatening to loose its bonds and free itself from the delicate airframe, it was all you could do not to lose all confidence in your ability to get her safely into the air *with* landing gear up, before she got all hot and bothered and blew a gasket.

But then, like a caiman slipping into water, it suddenly all made sense. Once you had the landing gear up, controlling the aircraft just feet off the ground with your left hand (thus taking it off the throttle!) working feverishly to get her how she wanted to be; wheels safely stowed, amber light on and thrumming into the blue, unshackled. And how.

She accelerated like nothing else, fast air rapidly soothing her angry radiators.

Then you could relax somewhat and enjoy, pressed back into the leather seat as you were with her eagerness. Revel. Let her do what she was born to do. Her hum sweetened, her temperature dropped along with your anxiety and you climbed steadily, to circle above a rapidly disappearing base that seemed to lessen in importance, in relevance, with every thousand foot Angel climbed.

To the left and right, your fellow pilots were arcing up with you as, at last, you finally witnessed the Shrew coming into her own, the sheer poetry of flight. There simply wasn't anything else to compare, certainly no words to describe. And yet. And yet, there was a solid, active denial in place, like some levered boulder, all but smothering a deep yearning to be back on that exact little plot of land, now no bigger than a matchbox. Back, sitting by the timeless fire, with a steaming mug of tea and a gifted cigarette. No point in looking down there. It would still be there later, whether you were or not. Base would miss you only in so much as the effort it took to replace you both.

.303 Browning Machine guns at the ready, poised behind their taut, red-painted calico covers, there to keep the guns clear and free of dirt, two Hispano 20mm cannon, two full tanks of fuel stacked in front of your chin, bullet-proofed glass clean, oxygen on. Checks on horizon, gyro, compass, rate of climb, altitude, fuel, temperature, thrust, prop set fine, we vectored to meet up with our bombers on the South coast, before heading out across the channel.

I had more hours under my belt than any other pilot in my detail. I had even taught one of them, so it felt even more imperative not to get shot down. I felt an overwhelming duty to be both an ambassador for Trinidad and a living example of Best Practice, as if, by being shot full of lead, I would somehow retrospectively besmirch the process of their education and thus, by extension, their belief in themselves and their own ability. It simply wasn't done for the teacher to prove so regrettably fallible. I had to be whiter than white. Getting nailed seemed to infer error on the pilot's behalf, especially in a Shrew; an aircraft so flagrantly superior to every other man-built contraption in the air.

It was rubbish of course. Men far better than me had been shot out of the sky, had made mistakes, had died. I had witnessed it with my own eyes. Sometimes you prayed that they would manage to get out, as their flying miracle twisted by seconds into a cremating coffin, plummeting leaden from the skies. Other times they exploded so quickly they wouldn't have known a thing about it. Luftwaffe numbers were truly awesome and many of their pilots superb, flying as they were inferior craft. I was convinced only the Poles really wanted to be up here.

The bombing raid over Amiens had progressed relatively smoothly. There was action as Gerry sent up some fighters to break up the run, but they were engaged before I had a chance myself to react to their arrival, positioned high, as I was. But, as we followed the inordinately stately crawl of the bombers on their final approach, we met with some unexpectedly fierce anti-aircraft fire.

Dirty black mushrooms blossomed and cracked around us and I marvelled at the poor bomber crew presenting as they did, much larger, sluggish, low altitude targets, against our much smaller, fleet-footed selves. Then, as we turned in a slow arc from the bomb run, we were bounced by 109's coming at us, unseen from the sun. We all split every which way, my number two thankfully breaking with me. I always taught never to fly more than 25 seconds in a straight line, rolling and dipping a crazy passage across the sky, as I strove to shake the two on my tail.

At speed, it was possible to pull a tight circle right at the edge of the Shrew's capability, until she started to judder, wanting to stall... and there, where you wanted to stall too, on the rim of a blackout, your vision first tunnelling and then starting to glaze over into a uniform grey, right there, your machine could do more than the Messerschmitt and could do it more *predictably*.

If you were able to allay the panic, familiar as you were with the territory, with the Lady at your toe, arse and fingertips, with your innate, God-given ability to fly, forbidding fear from swallowing your vital organs- your stomach, through your diaphragm clear through to your heart, from the pressure shrinking your eyeballs- then the Shrew would beat your pursuer, that fraction tighter in the turn and *then* it would be your go to turn pursuer.

Something I'd learned from my Polish counterparts that had quietly revolutionised my own approach to dog-fighting, was how they would wait patiently before hitting their adversary, wait until they were just a hundred or so feet from their quarry. The RAF had always taught pressing the button at around four hundred feet. Now even with four Browning .303's and two cannon, you were bereft of ammo in less than thirty seconds. That meant that quite apart from flying at well over 500mph in a dive, scanning the surrounding sky, keeping an eye on the rear view for possible assailants and correcting for deflection, you were expected to hit a fleeing aircraft hard enough -or well enough- to bring it down from a distance surpassing Wembley Football pitch.

But by pausing, by relying on the superior speed of a dive, or crazily approaching the enemy head on, driven on by no small measure of cold courage, what the Poles were doing in their Hurricanes was *filling* their gun target with enemy aircraft, so that -at one quarter the RAF Recommended Trigger Distance- it actually became hard to miss.   There remained though, a couple of drawbacks to this technique.

Subsequent to shooting down two enemy aircraft (which I confess had taken me a while), I figured I had balanced the books and anything else I snagged was a bonus, before being inevitably eliminated from the game. My own anxiety had been abated somewhat by the decision that I could relax, now that my existence in the Squadron, indeed the RAF, had been endorsed by these kills. My count was now five and a half; the half being a Heinkel 111 bomber I had finished that a Hurricane had started, back in December.

Having seen with my own eyes the success the Poles were having with their close-quarter method of combat, I had no qualms adopting it as my own. However, there was this catch. Any perceived sense of anxiety reduction I may have felt was more than offset by this new approach to gunning down the

Hun. Attacking head on meant that, more often than not, you were flying directly into their armament, whether they be fighter or bomber and, secondly, should you be successful in your gambit, head-on or not, the overriding concern then became how to avoid the incandescent mess you had just created of the unfortunate aircraft in front of you, close up and flying on a high speed collision course as you were.

I shook off one attacker and turned the tables on the other with my superior turning speed, managing to catch it and empty the last of my furious lead first into his starboard wing, across the cowling and then pump the Hispano into his fuselage, the Shrew shuddering with the extra-heavy cannon recoil. White glycol smoke plumed gratifyingly, but he dipped away, rather than down as I anticipated. No kill. Well, not a conclusive one, although I imagined he was going to have to land pretty sharpish, before his engine gave up the ghost on him.

I was precipitously near the ground, out of the theatre of combat and with no idea where I was and no sign of anyone else. No bombers and no fighters of either description, not even a vapour trail. I took in my fuel and then my compass, but compass and gyro were of course still spinning wildly from my extreme exertions. Using the sun, I pointed her nose to home. All seemed well, my concern now solely being how I got both of us safely back over friendly soil. And then it happened.

Chapter IV
2014

In that initial 'inert time' I had already envisaged quite clearly how his recovery was going to play out; how he would first come around enough to open his eyes and recognise who I was through a fog of pain, concussion and powerful painkillers. With his jaw wired up and every other limb and organ in his body attempting to recover, he wouldn't even be able to smile without experiencing discomfort, but the smile in his eyes and the tear that sprang out of the perfect corner of his eye, to be absorbed by the bandaging over his ear would be joy unbounded for me.

Over the following days we would then generate a simple system, where he would waggle the fingers on his good hand to signal most things and this, combined with the odd grunt, would pretty much cover the bulk of it. A bit like his teenage years to follow, no doubt. The original dread, looking over the precipice of what might possibly go wrong, or the notion of actually losing him would by then have receded and an adjusted normality replaced it, even though the situation was anything but.

I had taken a few days compassionate leave to get through the initial situation, thereafter shortening my days at work, meaning essentially no voluntary overtime. I was a joint director of the plastics engineering company I worked for, having set up with colleagues out of university, so there was a flexibility available to me that might not have been there if I wasn't a founder. I didn't allow the fortune of this fact any room to fester, as I sat in my customary position next to my prone boy.

The things that go through your head when you allow them rein; whole conversations, arguments, dialogues with people. How you wished you'd said something. How you imagined saying something in a forthcoming interchange. What they would say, how you would react. You'd think we'd have learned after the first few forays into this territory that it never works out that way in reality, yet still we persist.

After 24 hours, Tom's drip-fed sedation was switched off. He eventually came round and was 'appropriate, with no apparent deficit from the injury,' as the doctor would have it. Out of the woods then, as far as I was concerned.

I was holding Tom's good hand when he finally surfaced. After recognising me and then being examined, he drifted off to sleep again, never loosening his firm grip of my paw. Relief giving way to exhaustion, I rested my forehead on the edge of his high mattress and dropped off too. And as I did so, it was a familiar descent: too often my thoughts turned to the grimmer aspects of my recent past, before analgesic slumber found me.

Adoption is so hard. One doesn't choose to be adopted, one merely needs to appear suitably grateful for being chosen: That in the grim lottery of selection, you were fortunate to have all your limbs and functions in working order, with no discernible outward signs of debilitation. The problems it generates however, were destined to surface many years later. A bitter time capsule fingered down a baby's gaping throat, the chrysalis to a bug that, over ensuing years would pupate and quietly start to eat away at one's insides. Many would succumb; some to the emptiness it left behind, some would seek the self-medication of drugs or alcohol, some others would be consumed in entirety, by allowing the bug rein, until it outgrew the host, assuming their role in life. I knew now that the reason I chose the wife I chose was entirely because of the dysfunctional relationship I had with my adoptive mother and a deep-seated need to fix something that had gone so terribly wrong in the mists of my past. Seeking approval from a woman who had issues with men, the terror of abandonment preventing so many otherwise healthy relationships from ever getting off the ground; that wasn't standard, healthy behaviour.

I recalled a vivid dream I'd had at the time that had never left me. I was climbing Mount Rushmore, it was night, a strong Northwest wind was blowing and I was in only a white shirt, shoeless and my fingernails were torn and bleeding. As I pulled myself up the unyielding wall towards the familiar face above me, I realised I had been on this cliff face for years. Hand over hand, breathing hard, I forced myself on upwards, eventually negotiating the chin, then the overhang of the cheek, the worst part, too smooth for a proper finger-hold, my feet unable to find anything on which gain purchase, dangled useless beneath me. I was so tired, I just needed to relax my aching arms, just for a moment, but there was no respite. As I hung there, I realised why the face was familiar. It wasn't a US president, it was my wife, Bea. With renewed energy, a last desperate scramble I hoiked myself up to the smooth-stone ledge of her massive eyelid. Gripping with both hands, legs akimbo, I hauled myself up with all my remaining strength, intent on peering into the one eye, resolute that I would at last find an answer, unpick the puzzle, by finally being able to look into her soul. I pulled myself up, jamming a forearm on the ledge, the wind tearing angrily at me, but at last lifting my heavy head to gaze in, to see. But there was no soul. There was nothing there at all.

My leg kicked inadvertently, waking me up. Lifting my heavy head, I looked at his crooked arm. There was so much I needed to tell him: about slavery, about the subconscious, about death... but then surely it was important to speak more positively. About life then. Yes and about poetry. Tom already knew of the one poem I had known but lost. Verse of what it was to fly through sunlit clouds made 'Cathedrals in the Sky'. It was important he had a positive aspect going into his future, so he would be attracted by and to the positive in life. My head already back down, I closed my eyes.

Just six hours later and he was cogent. In fact he could talk surprisingly well, he just preferred not to. Another day and he was sat up in bed and aware of all that was going on around him. He apologised for the accident and for destroying his bike, which was indeed the case. The young lady with the dog had taken care of the remains. He had managed to straighten the forks, crush the front wheel and bend the frame, which was a not inexpensive Genesis Titanium. Of course, none of this really mattered, as he was on the mend. And so, with the prospect of some hours before us and an essentially captive audience, albeit I suspected, a potentially willing one for what I was about to expound, I made a start.

"Tom" I said. He could immediately tell from my tone that I was about to launch into something important to him and transferred what must have been a quite considerable proportion of his attention onto the space that followed that single syllable, left hanging in the vortex between us. Unused as I was to this unexpected occurrence, it made what I was struggling to begin that much harder. An immediate pressure to then say something totally meaningful, earning the unexpected power I had managed to command when I elected to start this conversation, at least temporarily threatened to overwhelm me.

As I had considered the commencement of regaling The Tale of Dad on my recent well-trod journey to St Mary's, I had pictured myself just easing into it seamlessly, so he wouldn't even notice the join and we would be ten days in and half way through it before he clocked that I was, in fact, telling him my life story, The Parable of Dad; the one thing he had -at least recently anyway- always wanted to know.

But here, now, I had just said 'Tom…' as I must have uttered a million times before and suddenly, this tantamount immobile boy had managed to convey, with just the merest of movements, an almost complete transformation, such a transference in weight of concentration, that I was shocked and thus terrified that whatever I did or said next, it would prove an all-embracing let down and I would lose him forever to one of his many screens.

I had been just about invisible before, invisible and silent, or so it seemed for all the heed he paid my parenthood. God. It had all started to slide even by the age of two. He was still there when I resurfaced, his eyes unblinking, as round as bright, painted saucers, looking at my face with such intent, as if for the first time. I realised I had absolutely no idea how long I'd been silent.

"I was wondering whether you thought it might be a good idea..." his fingers twitched quizzically, with a grunt

"What?"

"...Whether or not you might be interested... no, no, no..."

"What?" he said, the menace much enhanced by clenched teeth.

Ok, I was milking it, but I had him now, I knew I had him hooked and I also knew that the payoff would be worth it too. It gave me such a delicious, huge inner grin I couldn't help myself.

"Well, as you're sitting there and will be for some time to come and I'm sat here with you, I was wondering whether you might be. At all interested in. hearing a little story... About. A. Certain. Spitfire!"

The moment I finished saying that last word, I regretted to the Centre of my Living Soul what I had just done. No (sane) parent ever wishes pain upon any child, particularly their own, but the bolt of unalloyed, ecstatic joy that I had just so successfully delivered on that poor lad would of course inevitably have to be expressed physically, as any child does, be it jumping up and down, throwing themselves on the floor, or hugging the life out of you.

He tried to start at least two of these, but the instantaneous resulting wattage of pain that ramped through every nerve and sinew in his body, the pain that had been sitting in the wings beside me, like a motionless, cresting tidal wave, patiently biding its time in the shadows, silent but ever threatening, got to have another go at his wracked frame; it must have been even more powerful than the moment he had received all of his blessed injuries in the first place and I, I had delivered it. His monitor started flashing.

"Oh God, Tom.. I'm So sorry. I'm so Sorry.. I didn't mean to do that to you." Through all of this, he had hardly moved at all, only letting out a barely audible sigh, but to anyone tuned in to him even half as much as I was, that split-second journey from Focus, to Joy, to the quintessence of heart-stopping, breath-taking Pain was as massive as a five act opera. And I include the full orchestra. Helpless, I watched him recover, lashing my brain with a birch for being so damned stupid and self-centred not to have thought it through. I realised I would have caused him less pain if I'd said nothing at all and just tipped him out of bed. It meant a careful reassessment of how I unfolded the story to him. Neither of us could afford to go through that again.

"I'm a pillock."

Tom lay frozen, just his laboured breathing and a zigzagging line on the monitor betraying the seismal enormity of what had just happened. It was clear even minutes later that the pain had still not subsided much. And he was exhausted. To top off my humiliation, a nurse arrived, sweeping the curtain aside and sliding over to the monitor with practiced speed, her brow a crease of puzzlement. She looked at Tom, then the monitor, then Tom again, prodded the monitor buttons and then made some adjustments to his drip.

I realised, somewhat belatedly, that his monitors must have been hooked up to some other computer and I had actually managed to trip an alarm, like some lush in a minefield. Finally, she turned her attention to me. I had hoped that if I sat still enough for long enough, if I breathed really lightly, one ankle locked around the chair leg to prevent movement, whilst also delivering guilt-pain and discomfort to my ankle, I would remain completely invisible and everything would swiftly return to normal.

I was mistaken. Like mothers, nurses have a Sixth Sense. 'Perhaps it's time for Tom to catch up on some rest' was all she said, but the waves of admonishment, disapproval and concern were enough to knock out a pillbox at fifty paces and have me melting for the exit faster than grease on a waffle iron. Anyway, she was in all probability, a mother too.

What a tit. All those heroic thoughts of giving my child what he needed most; attention, love and guidance as to the way forward for this growing lad, through the jungle of years that lead to mature adulthood and all I had successfully managed to deliver was one very singular round with Mike Tyson.

Home without my boy was far harder than expected, even for 48 hours. Most of the time he was there, I realised, he was creating a disturbance to the force-field that was my own existence. The endless washing up, the clearing up, the laundry, the phone calls, the arrangements, the changes to arrangements, lost football boots, lost phones, lost money, lost keys(!), the noise, the smell, the interruption. As I sat now in my warm, calm, uninterrupted silence, I understood what a terrible, selfish, stupid father I was. He had the patience of a Saint to cope with me.

The next time I went, looking around somewhat furtively, lest the same nurse be on duty, I found him already occupied with two schoolmates, Cosmo and Trent. Having bobbed around in the background, signalling to him in improvised Hospital Semaphore 'not to worry' and 'I would be off', I went to make another swift exit, but a flick of his head stopped me obediently in my tracks and I watched as, again, he communicated easily with his brethren.

He had a way of listening that I recognised and was grateful for. But the boys conversation had inevitably been curtailed, or at least stunted, by my uncool arrival and, despite my protestations for the boys to stay longer, they soon bid their farewells (well, that was my take on it, I feel they would have expressed their exit differently) and left. As they passed me, I enquired after them and whether they were alright getting home, but they tarried only long enough to be polite, nodded in the right places and then made their intended escape.

I turned and looked at Tom nervously, expecting admonishment. As if I was suddenly the boy and he the adult. When he was very young, there had been a period where he had had this imperious air about him, when he was being transported on my back in a carrier, or in the car seat, he always gave off this feeling that everyone about him were his minions, going about their business purely to serve and delight him, whether he knew them or not.

But there was no punishment forthcoming, only a relaxed air of expectancy. He waded motionlessly through all my small talk, as a man passing through a field of tall reeds, patient, but looking forward to getting to the other side and on with more salient matters. All he knew of this story, as far as I was aware, was that as a child of twelve, I had rebuilt a

Spitfire engine with my own hands and all I ever wanted was to fly in one. And the poem. He knew about the poem. However, it wasn't quite as straightforward as that. I mean really though, when the Hell is it?

I seem to remember spending almost all of my childhood studying the ground. Wherever I walked, wherever I went, the floor always held an endless fascination for me. Perhaps because as a baby you have such an intimate relationship with it and then, growing up, you remain so much closer to it than you are as an adult, you also never think anything at all of flinging yourself wholeheartedly on it, no matter what it might comprise of at the time. It's your friend, it's immediate and is always tossing up the new, the unexpected. Besides, any adult you were with always seemed to be occupied with things that went on 'up there', which very much left you to your own devices down at ground level.

As a consequence of this time-consuming study of my terrain, I found money on many occasions and not just pennies, but even fivers and one time, a small bag with two tenners in it. I also found foreign coins, pins, badges, plastic soldiers, bits of an aeroplane, a kite, elastic bands, stones, pebbles (there is a difference), crystals, fossils, shells, expended fireworks, dead sparklers, interesting bits of wood, leaves, fir cones (open and closed), cards, playing cards, pellets, spent shotgun cartridges, key-rings, fake jewellery, acorns, conkers, clay pipes, old bottles, flints, bottle-tops, ring-pulls, string, bicycle tyre valves, nuts, bolts, screws, corks, buckles, lids, hooks, lead shot, pots, a magnifying glass, magnets, marbles, ball bearings, grommets, puffballs, tennis balls, batteries, o-rings, padlocks, eyeliner, laces, jet-balls and, spectacularly, a watch.

Then there was all the live stuff. Ants, ladybirds, crabs, frogs, grasshoppers, daddy longlegs, snails, slugs, buttercups, daisies, worm-casts (not technically live, I grant you), worms, beetles, earwigs, Devils coach horse beetles, silverfish, fleas, woodlice, hedgehogs, money spiders, moths, butterflies, centipedes, millipedes, slow worms and even a grass snake. Finders' Keepers' was King. Neighbours pets didn't count.

For the most part, when accompanied, all of the treasures I found were batted out of my hand almost as fast as I could pick them up by a mother concerned only in the perceived cleanliness of the current object of my ardour. Nevertheless, I still managed to accrue quite a collection in small cardboard boxes and on the windowsill of my room, arranged in changeable order of ascending majesty.

Things that were super-special often tended to stay in ones pockets though. So it wouldn't be unheard of to travel to school, or indeed out to play, with some basic essentials, like string, obviously, but then a dog whistle, a conker, a cork, several collectible bubble-gum wrappers, an elastic band (the bigger the better), marbles (several you played with and a special one only for show), a penknife (if you had one), a bullet (if you had one), a jet-ball, a pen, maybe a soldier, a toy car and some coinage of the realm for trips to the tuckshop or corner store (if you had any) and anything new or exotic to show off, like a foreign coin. Pockets never seemed quite big enough, really. Not when you considered what you had to leave behind.

I've no idea how it is now, but things like bullets were never live and tended to be acquired either by very skilful 'swapsies', although certain items such as bullets tended never to be on the swapsie list, or from Air Shows like Duxford, where (social misfit) Demigods would have stalls that sold outsized model planes and war paraphernalia… such as bullets. They would also have things like unfeasibly ferocious, multi-purpose bowie knives, machine gun belts and even hand grenade casings.

These stalls would have a permanent but shifting army of children, captivated by their lofty treasures, fingering shell casings and rusty magazines with a hushed, glistening solemnity that any Sunday church would pay for. The only other place to source this sort of thing would be older Air Cadets, who got to use the firing ranges and secreted cartridges or spent rounds out in their socks.

I have a theory that as boys, we are almost solely focussed on destruction; destruction in the best, biggest, or most clinical fashion. It didn't matter whether it was deftly removing the carefully applied soft putty from the brand new windows of a newly built house, slicing the heads off flowers with a perfectly whippy switch, killing ants, be it by magnifying glass, or elastic band. Killing flies, pulling the legs off daddy longlegs, shooting things, putting bangers in tulips, pulling up saplings, snapping branches, breaking eggs, smashing flowerpots, knocking down walls, cracking the code, breaking the lock… everything that could be was tested to destruction, or simply destroyed.

But at some point in life, this need to be The Ultimate Destroyer, the ninja, or soldier, or superhuman, the Harbinger of Death and Destruction of All who would Stand Before transforms, all being well, during his teenage years. And all that energy and exactitude then gets funnelled in to *creating* things, with the same technical application and attention to detail. With Lego and then Meccano.

Electronic Sets give rise to Crystal Radios, to burglar alarms… and Science Kits to crystal gardens and indoor fireworks and thus the interest beyond… This amazing thing happens, as must have happened across the Ages of Man, where annoying little boys with whom nothing is safe, who should be seen but not heard, suddenly come out of their chrysalis, years later, having invented something extraordinary, like the steam engine, the gyroscope, or the sewing machine. Or discovered gravity, electricity, or the muon.

So much of this brilliant potential energy is now focussed in a wholly artificial way, into videogames. These boys are being tricked, sold short, but it's still a lesser evil for many an overwrought parent. Their kids are safe indoors, not 'out there' of an evening, running amok, causing mischief, or susceptible to those that would do harm or lead them astray. But all of that energy is poured into the virtual world, still killing, still maiming and striving to gain levels and the respect of their peer community.

But these games offer up nothing new, nothing not already designed by someone else and thereby reduced by definition. There is no 'random' in there, no gaps filled by true imagination, no chasm through which to fall and thereby find oneself. No nature. No true discovery. The emptiness is not verdant.

Beyond sharpening reflexes and some peer respect, what positive gain is there for the child of this gift? The argument is there, is clear and unequivocal, but who wants to hear it? Not me. Not my son. But presently, one arm strapped and no sudden movements, his mind slides around, ravenous for a finger hold, now that so much is denied him. No Xbox, nor PSP, even a Kindle seems awkward, one handed.

"Hello Tom. How are you feeling?" he waved an arm with a listless 'so so, I'm bored with this' sensibility. I take my customary chair. He's had a pocket mirror taped to the arm of his TV so he can look at anyone sitting in the chair without constantly craning his neck. It also means, he can have the TV on and if the company bores him, he can watch the screen, which he's happy to do even with the sound down and still at least appear to be engaging with his guest.

Then he remembered something.

"Have you had a phone call at all?"

"What do you mean, a phone call?" I said. I'd had a million phone calls. "From Whom?" I always tried to speak correctly when with him. For no other reason than to provide a proper role model, I guess. Maybe it was silly. He searched my face for a moment, with more than a hint of mischief on his own.

"No one." He said, confirming my suspicions. I knew better than to try and elicit any more information head on. But he had me thinking. I scrolled mentally through the messages on my voicemail, both mobile and landline over the last day or two. Eliminating work, expected calls from school,

Bridget, the Police, the driver and lady who had witnessed the accident and taken the bike, friends, responses to the rearrangement of my diary... no, nothing out of the ordinary. Nothing unexpected, nothing that would warrant the smirk on this boy's chops.

I didn't give him anything. It was imperative, when playing this game, as his humour had evolved, not to show weakness. Total unconcern was the order of the day, but I confess he had me pronged fair and square on the antlers of the elk he'd just shoved in the room.

I refocused back on him to see if there might be any other morsel of information to be gleaned on the situation. His eyes were shut and, for a moment, I thought he was feigning either sleep or disinterest to prevent any further probing on my behalf, but even as I thought that, the monitors began to flash. As I rose, a nurse swiftly appeared, scanning the machine and Tom.

Things moved really fast from there. He was wheeled away by a barrage of people and then a doctor came and spoke very quickly to me. I made a mental decision not to try and understand what he was saying to me, but memorize exactly what he said, word for word.

Chapter V
1976

I was awoken at an inhuman hour yet again by an imperfect cockadoodle-doo emanating from the hen house and cursed the bird, wondering if I could persuade Grandad to sort him out for Sunday roast, as he was of course going to be doing that every morning. Rolling my head under the pillow, I resigned myself to the fact that my minutes there were numbered. The curtain swung bodily, obscuring another bright day and it was clear from the sounds and smells coming up from the kitchen, Gran's dog conversations and scuffed footsteps in the yard that I was the last up and by some way.

Shuffling down for breakfast, in stark contrast to home, the table was laid with a brightly embroidered cloth with fresh-baked brown bread, sized similarly to a house-brick and equally as challenging to get past the crust. Once inside however, it was moist, warm and tasty. Goats milk to drink and pour on my Weetabix and eggs galore. Grandma enquired from the kitchen whether I wanted a duck egg. Why not? They were huge and tasted amazing. Strawberry jam on toast rounded it all off and I dutifully, if unwillingly, sidled into the kitchen to see if I could be of service.

This was Grandma's domain. A complex and multi-layered program of pots, pans, cloths, utensils, buckets, basins, plates, cups, mugs, cutlery and foodstuffs all competing for space against whole, dead poultry, greens, fresh spuds awaiting a rinse, clean spuds, pot plants on the windowsill, opened post somewhat incongruously in a bowl with the house keys and fresh fruit, teapots, coffee pots, a baby kid goat expecting a feed and the washing suspended from the ceiling on a hanging pulley drier. Accordingly, there were always many juxtaposed smells competing for attention, but the overriding two tended to be the pungent smell of washing outpunching the baking.

You never touched anything in the kitchen without explicit permission to do so. Grandma handed me a wicker hand basket and instructed me to collect the eggs as usual; cue to vacate the kitchen. I knew from past experience that the chickens were a canny bunch and didn't necessarily lay them at all where you might expect, so I set off across the back yard, firstly taking in the hay barn, before heading down the slight hill to the hen house.

It proved a good move, as I found three there and another two in the hedge on the way to the coop, where I retrieved another six. The stink inside the hen house always assaulted my central heating sensibilities and I tended to do as much as I could with breath held, although this tended to be impossible, due to the time it took to do the job thoroughly. You couldn't rush egg collection. I always felt a little uncomfortable divesting chickens of their eggs, like a brazen burglar, not even caring that the homeowners were standing there helpless, whilst I helped myself to the crown jewels. No wonder they resorted to finding alternative nesting places.

Before coming to the farm, I'd never really looked properly at a chicken. Boy, they were funny birds. Couldn't even fly. I remembered a Ladybird book read to me about a chicken and a fox, but I could not for the life of me remember anything of the story. I just remember the chicken being unfeasibly red in the pictures. These ones were red, but less so and they were just the most extraordinary shape, pretty big and totally un-aerodynamic, as far as I could see. There was also the offending iridescent-green tailed white cockerel, who really did lord it about the place. A couple of hens scratched about in the earth and pecked. A couple more were content to sit on perches, feathers ruffled up, making them look super comfortable.

When I would turn up and feed them, they really were ready for the food and scrabbled over each other with much sound and fury to get to it. Part of their food mix also meant feeding them yesterday's eggshells. I couldn't quite believe that they would be cannibal enough to eat them, but Gran insisted I do it, saying it helped the chickens make strong, healthy new ones. Certainly, they attacked the shells with as much gusto as the floury feed, veg and breadcrumbs.

The ducks were left to their own devices at night, presumably because unlike a chicken, they could fly away from any trouble, stay in the pond or on the island, safe from foxes. Despite all this, the more time I spent with them, the more I grew to like the chickens. They seemed to have a very strong sense of who they were. I closed the roof to the hen house and looked out across the fields. It wasn't great not being at home, but it wasn't bad here either. Upon returning, Grandma was gratifyingly impressed with my egg haul and suggested I ring Mum and see how she was.

I did so from the relative quiet of the lounge, where I found Hamlet sprawled across the hearthrug, successfully managing to take up most of the room in the process. A hugely friendly animal, he was just so inordinately big. He raised his head, his impressive mouth lolling open as I entered, but immediately slumped back down from the exertion, losing interest as soon as he clocked me. He was entirely devoted to Grandma and really wasn't interested in anything else that anyone else did, unless it involved chow. This made him an efficient guard dog however, as his sole self-allotted purpose in life, apart from eating fantastical quantities of food, was to safeguard Grandma from any harm.

This meant that anyone approaching the farm got a stiff reception from Dracula's dog, bounding up to them at speed. I had seen Sixteenth Century warhorses in full battledress that somehow seemed less imposing than Hamlet. He could also detect Gran from extraordinary distances. He could somehow determine the correct car tone, distinguishing it from all others, whilst the car was still half a mile away, long before it reached even the end of the drive.

All of the farm animals there were kind of remarkable. The ducks, geese, cats, chickens, pigs, goats and dog all seemed to understand how things were and worked together in complete harmony, even if that meant just maintaining a respectful distance, but they all also seemed to be a bit larger than life. The chickens really were large, not at all scrawny. Their eggs bigger and tastier than the ones we had from the supermarket at home.

The cats were semi-feral and pretty much lived and bred in the hay barn, producing litters of kittens that all needed a home. It took a great deal of time and patience to actually get to stroke a cat and even then, you would only get lucky with one or two. The others had no time or saw no point in the pursuit, although if you did manage to catch one on its own, it was more likely to let you. I wasn't convinced Gran or Grandad were completely sure how many they had. I certainly hadn't been told all their names. Feeding consisted filling five saucers with tinned food. They found their own water.

One of the mother cats, Suki, was a master (mistress?) hunter(ess). Not only did she sort out any rats that figured they might set up a home in one of the barns or outbuildings, but once, she even managed to bring down a seagull. I didn't see the event itself, but found the evidence one morning behind the greenhouse, when I went round to retrieve the pig feed. It looked like a murder scene, all blood and flattened undergrowth, but no bird. Just the careful outline in disturbance and bloodied feathers of where a spread-eagled seagull had once been, as if laid out on a cross. I mean, that's impressive; they're sizeable birds, wielding fearsome beaks.

What makes a cat, lying in the sun, watching the world go by, think 'Hey, that seagull there, I can take it. I know I can.' Amazing. I don't think any of the other cats would even have contemplated it. They might've looked on, their bodies tensing, tail-tip twitching, jaw all aquiver at the thought of it, but Suki would happily have stalked wildebeest, if they'd ever strayed into the bottom field. Surveying Hamlet's imposing bulk, I sat in the lounge and dialled home but, after letting it ring twelve times to no answer, replaced the receiver.

I wandered slowly back upstairs, wondering what to do, with no telly and no mates. Halfway up, they had a bookshelf, mostly with a load of uninteresting guff: The Adventures of Robin Hood, Tom Sawyer, Huckleberry Finn, The Jungle Book, Grimm's Fairy Tales, but there was a newer paperback, The Machine Gunners, and then some dusty poetry books. I weighed up whether it was possible to remove a book and it not be noticed as missing.

Being caught by Gran stair-surfing on a thin sun lounger mattress effectively banned me from playing in the house at all and I was consigned thereafter to the playroom and the Den at the end. These were part of a barn conversion, annexed to the main house. The Den had an ancient, massive, busted TV in it and lots of musty old sofas and cushions. You might sometimes find a cat in there, but he would more often than not slip out, the moment you walked in.

The larger playroom infront had a table tennis table as a permanent fixture in the middle, a couple of bare paddles and even some balls, though they were only one star, but the total highlight, sitting in the far corner of the room up against the Den partition, was a working jukebox that didn't even need money. You just switched it on at the wall, waited a while for it to warm up and then chose what you wanted. There was other stuff, Jazz, Country and Western, Disco, but that was my introduction to Queen's 'Seven Seas Of Rye'. To David Bowie and to Supertramp's masterful 'Crime Of The Century' album; 'Dreamer', 'Rudy' and 'School' slowly being replaced as favourites by 'Asylum'.

You just committed yourself to thumb-pressing two big, plastic buttons to select your record and the machinery went into action, the catalogue in the back rotated around with a hum and then a semi-circular arm went in and extracted the chosen 45', pulled back, simultaneously turning through 90 degrees and placed it on the small turntable.

I noted that the centres of all the discs had been punched out, enabling the jukebox to locate the records easily over a fat, spinning cone in the middle. Then, the arm retracted as the needle hit the first groove with a crackle and bump, amplified out across the speakers spread around the room and then, the soft strum of 'Starman' would fill the air and I would stand transfixed, hands gently resting on the chrome of the jukebox, watching the warped vinyl ripple round unevenly, as first the drums and then the vocals finally cut in.

If I was honest, I hadn't a clue what 'boogie' was, but if I knew anything, I suddenly understood in the core of my being, that all the children absolutely needed to be allowed to boogie. All of them. And me especially; at the front, leading the boogie. He wasn't even human, but man, could he play guitar.

Those early days, I had thought I might have to avoid Grandad, but there was simply no sign of him from morning to evening. He would be there at dinner, taking up his customary position at the head of the table, where he would sit in some sort of quiet meditation, the tips of his fingers pressed together infront of him, elbows resting on the arms of his heavy chair. His was the only one with arms, so no one else could affect this posture with any sense of ease, even if they felt like it.

The first couple of evenings, he didn't have anything to say to me, although he would sometimes look at me over a steaming bowl of potatoes, or such. I couldn't work out his expression, preferring to avert my eyes if I thought this was about to change.

One particular day, I had been exploring much further afield, past the limits of the farm, across a track and into the woods beyond. The land was beginning to look pretty parched from the extended hot weather and the whole place seemed to be mysteriously overrun with ladybirds. I had read about plagues and they were absolutely everywhere. It was going to be a long summer.

I climbed up a friendly oak tree and sat there for some time, eventually eliciting the interest of a robin that seemed intent on getting to know me. I immediately wondered what they ate. If it was ladybirds, he was going to have a family of thirty. Watching him in action, it became clear that his domain was the hedge. He would constantly hop around inside it, presumably looking for food and maybe even building a nest somewhere within that secret world, veiled to any passer-by through the outer layer of leaves and made impenetrable due to the close-packed branches within.

There were some other birds making a racket in some tall trees above and behind me. I wasn't sure if they were crows or rooks. Or ravens. I didn't think they were ravens. Two rabbits appeared at the bole of a nearby tree and nibbled the young grass there. All was peace until I was threatened by a thing that ought to have been a wasp, but seemed much bigger and harder. As I ducked from its space-crowding approach on my face, I very nearly lost my balance, experiencing momentary vertigo, causing me to panic and hold on to the branch until I calmed down. Perhaps it wasn't a great idea to be up a tree. And I should have brought a book, but I hadn't thought to bring anything from home.

Things had been tense with Mum for quite some time. It hadn't been so bad for a while, but I was at a really white school and was getting picked on especially by two guys. One of them, Probert was really hard. He was two years older, much bigger than me and generally violent. It was like there was something missing in his brain, which allowed him this sort of fearless, reckless, awesome confidence, like he was above the law and all the rules that governed other people. Word was he'd also had an operation to have his tear ducts removed, so he couldn't even cry. Maybe that was why he was fearless.

Any which way, he would hold me to ransom every day he could find me.

"Handover, Pakocurry."

I would hand over my lunchbox, which he would tear open to retrieve the Penguin biscuit, thrusting it into my face.

"What you doin' with white people's food? Why don't you eat curry, Pakocurry? You can't eat this. You ain't allowed." He would then toss my sandwiches across the road, finally to spit in the blue Tupperware before throwing it back at me. The ritual became boring after a while, meaning I would have to go to the school toilets to flush the box under a tap. It also meant I got very hungry, come lunchtime.

But when your own family don't properly understand racism, because they're white, then you can't take that sort of thing home and tell your parents. Or anyone, really. There was one other black kid at the school, in a different year from me, but when we saw each other, there was this unspoken understanding that passed between us, imperceptible to anyone else. We would never be friends, but we both knew.

I knew I had withdrawn from Mum. She used to say 'at least we have each other' and we would sit together in the evenings, snuggled up watching the telly. But now, I didn't feel like it. I wasn't a kid anymore. I knew she missed it, but I didn't know what to say. I didn't want to do it, that was all. I felt bad, but we all have shit to deal with, right? I also felt that she would sense my shame, the shame I was feeling for being bullied every day and I felt a need to protect her from that. But if I got too close, she would know somehow. Smell it on me and start causing a fuss, or something. I couldn't have her walking me to school, or even worse, phoning the Head.

Even some teachers weren't above picking you out. Humiliating you. Wrinkling their noses distastefully, like you'd stepped in dog shit, or just laughing with the rest of the class when someone asked if you were 'browned off' about some other invisible infraction. Any given class could catch you unawares at any time, when the subject of study would cover topics as diverse as rubber manufacture, American History, the sugar trade, spices, rice, elephants, The Raj, world populations, famine and flood appeals, the cotton industry, Mount Everest, religion... the potential for some crushing witticism was endless and any foothold gained was always temporary. Even if you scored a point in class, perhaps by answering a question correctly, you more than paid for it in the corridor after, at break.

Lighting fires just seemed to take some of the pressure off, like a stress relief. Like doing something so secret and so naughty, that positively no one else knew about, somehow made it better, at least for a while. Just the way the flame would start, almost invisible for a second, like it had died as you introduced the match to the tinder. Then, you cupped your hands, so no gust of wind would get to it and gradually, it would grow along an edge of dry leaf, or spread like a black stain across a nest of dead grass, or travel along the edge of a piece of paper, growing longer and larger by the second, until you just had to back away, as the smoke started to unfurl and the fire really take.

At first, it was about the set up, then it became about scarpering. Not being caught. There was a gut level excitement to it all, from the start. Recceing a possible target, checking you weren't being observed from any angle, lighting the match, all the time your stomach tight, as you looked around for adults who might clock you, or kids who would grass you up.

But out here, I didn't feel like I wanted to start a fire. It was funny. There were matches in the kitchen and even a green cigarette lighter in the Den, but I hadn't even thought to pick it up.

I knew Mum was ill, but I didn't know what to do about it. I had a feeling somehow it was all my fault. I mean, if I had just been better, not so naughty, maybe God wouldn't have punished me so badly.

Three things had gone wrong in quick succession. I managed to smash a light in the school hallway by slamming a jetball into the floor, where it immediately shot up and knocked a fluorescent lamp clean off the ceiling. The plastic cover didn't hit anyone, which was lucky, because it was pretty hefty and definitely might have killed someone, but I really smashed it and glass just showered everywhere, in people's hair and everything. If no one had been there, except maybe two mates to witness it, it would have been so cool. I don't even know who grassed me, but it was probably loads of people and probably girls. They're so stupid.

That morning, I'd been in the playground and one of my tricks was to bite the inside of my cheek, suck a gobbet of blood into my mouth, then spit it out in the playground. I was doing just that when the Deputy Head, her attention caught by my small audience, witnessed my act from a first floor window. I didn't know anything was up until she collared me on the way back in and asked me first if I was ill and when I told her 'no', she asked me to explain exactly what it was I had been doing.

I described the procedure and, after thinking a moment, she told me it was 'disgusting' and 'not to do it again, ever'. I think she was looking to take things further, but fortunately at that moment, she got side-tracked by two girls who had got into a fight because one had called the other a 'cow'.

I'd then kind of forgotten about that until this jetball incident happened and found myself hauled out of Metalwork to sit outside the Head's office waiting to go in. I liked Metalwork. The teacher had a huge beard and was cool. As I sat there, the Deputy Head came by, going to her office and I saw she was holding my satchel. I'd left it on the radiator at the break when I was bouncing the jetball and she, intending to take it to lost property, had opened it to find out whose it was.

She then came across one of my phials full of meths and turps. So, with that, I had to sit for an hour whilst my Mum was called to the school to listen to me explain myself, not just to her and the Head, but the Deputy Head as well. She was a racist. She sat there, loving every minute of it.

Thankfully, they never worked out the true significance of the phials, but they knew they were missing several from the Science labs. This on its own would probably have been enough but, coupled with the blood-gobbing incident and the jetball escapade, they felt had no option but to 'suspend me with immediate effect' while they 'reviewed the matter', with the distinct possibility that I 'would be asked to leave the school'. No one actually said 'expelled' at any point. Like even the word was too terrible to be spoken.

I think if my Mum had been at full strength, she wouldn't have taken it all so badly, but all the way home, I was expecting her to say something, to get really angry and pinch my ear 'til it burned, but she didn't. She stayed silent the whole journey. We just sat in the car and drove and she didn't look at me once. So I knew, once we got back that it wouldn't be like normal.

I went upstairs, changed and then went down again to say sorry. I found her in the kitchen, she was crouching, leaning against the cupboard and crying so hard, in a way I'd never seen. I put my arm around her and told her I was really, truly sorry, but she was crying so much she couldn't even speak. Then she sent me down the road on my bike to get us fish and chips. I was so alarmed at first I didn't want to go, but she insisted, pushing her purse into my hand.

When I got back, she was normal again, but very quiet and her face looked blasted. We ate the fish and chips out of their wrappers, instead of using plates and then she said that she had 'let me down' and I said that I had 'let her down', but she just looked at me. After a pause where I knew something else was coming, the thing I had been waiting for in the car, she said she wasn't able to cope anymore and it wasn't me, it was her. I would have preferred it if she *had* smacked me. Then she told me she had breast cancer.

And then I realised I was crying really hard, holding my fork in my fist really hard and wishing I could stab it in the Deputy Head's face, really hard. Then she told me about going to stay with Gran and Grandad, 'just for a while, 'til she had managed to sort herself out.' Now, I wanted to stay with her, I just wanted to stay there with her and look after her, but she said I couldn't do that and it was best I went down to Kent for a while. And that I was to be on 'best behaviour all the time I was down there.'

And then we hugged each other really hard and we cried. I've never cried so hard for so long. And I held her face in my hands and kissed her cheeks and forehead and nose and told her I loved her and that it would all be alright, but she'd made up her mind.

Chapter VI
1976

Somewhere overhead I could hear the soft, throbbing whine of a plane and climbed higher up to see if I could catch sight of it through the branches. The deep, throaty roar got louder and louder, then zoomed straight over my head, disappearing quickly behind the tree cover. I could swear it was a Spitfire though. It was low enough to make out the shape and the roundel on the underside of the wing. Cool.

I dug into my dinner, but just as I had stuffed a forkful, carefully stacked with pork, potato and gravy into my grateful mouth, Grandad turned his full attention to me.

"So, what have you been doing with yourself?" The mouthful actually gave me a few minutes to calm the panic of a seasoned truant and compose what I regarded as a considered answer.

"I got the eggs and I went exploring. Do you have a rabbit snare?" I said.

"A rabbit snare? You want to catch rabbits?"

"Yes. I'll need a snare and some carrots from the garden." I said. Answering with a question was always a good idea.

"Carrots, indeed." He looked at Grandma. "Well, I can see if I have a snare, but you can't have any carrots. They get quite enough as it is."

"So, what should I use instead?" I asked. I mean, what else would you catch a rabbit with?

"Oh that's easy," he said. "Just go and make a noise like a carrot."

'A noise like a carrot'? I pondered this. What the Hell kind of noise does a carrot make? I resolved to go and listen to the carrots in the garden the very next day. Perhaps the tops, when they blew in the wind made a whistle-y sound. He interrupted my train of thought.

"Did you see the plane fly over?"

"The Spitfire?! Yes, it went straight over my head. It was really low."

"I think it might have been a Hurricane." He said. "But it's an easy mistake to make."

"Oh." I said. I wasn't convinced. After all, what did he know? It went straight over my head, after all.

"Probably on its way back from a flying display." He continued. I carried on eating. Then Grandma chipped in. Normally, she would only say things that pertained to everyday topics, like food, or washing, or my mum, so I was surprised when she said-

"Do you know what your grandfather did during the War?" I shook my head, wisely having timed another huge mouthful of food, precluding a more wordy response.

"He was an aero-engineer." She said, somewhat proudly. I looked across the table's expanse to him, hoping that he might elucidate, giving me more of a clue exactly what that meant before I had to speak again.

"He used to fix Spitfires when they came back from fighting." I swallowed painfully, almost choking in my impatience to get the next word out.

"Really?"

"Yes, really." With that, she went back out to the kitchen with a serving dish. I looked back at him again.

"You mended Spitfires in the War?"

He smiled a half smile, which might have been 'no, it's just a joke', but I suspected it was actually more of a 'why yes, of course'. I couldn't believe my Mum had never told me. The picture hanging up behind his head then leapt out, almost clubbing me over the bonce. It was a very plain black-and-white pencil drawing I had never taken the slightest notice of before, but suddenly it demanded I look at it. It was a Spitfire flying out from behind two towering clouds.

Life Before Me never really made that much sense, at least not in terms of Gran and Grandad. I understood History and all that, of course, but up until that point, Gran and Grandad simply existed to be Gran and Grandad to me. That was their sole purpose. And the Den, the playroom, this farm, everything, was basically there to service me. But now, just in that one smile, suddenly it all transmogrified and I understood something for the first time; the concept that they had had a life before me. That they had once been young and played and climbed trees and fallen in love and had a child and that child was my Mum, who couldn't have children, so she had adopted me, even though I was brown and she wasn't.

I mean, I had known all this before, but I hadn't *known* it. Not properly. I ate the rest of my dinner in silence, stunned and totally occupied in the digesting of my own epiphany and all that it entailed, as much as anything of my meal. I think it kind of took the wind out of Grandad's sails a bit, because from there on, he kept looking over in my direction expectantly, as if now ready to answer the million questions that I was going to fire at him about the War and Spitfires and everything. Only I didn't.

I did however, move through the house with new eyes, picking out things I had previously neglected to notice. Bits of paper framed on the walls that turned out to be letters, or tickets, or certificates, sepia pictures of airmen and planes, or huts. Some of them might even have been Grandad, but it was impossible to know. Pictures of bits of engines.

Many of the previously faceless, ancient hardback tomes with gold lettering on the spine turned out to be engineering manuals or books about flying. The pages were yellowed with age and the pictures always black-and-white illustrations, rarely even photos, but all of them were crammed with engineering info. I could read an engineering drawing. That was something we had done in Metalwork.

After our initial introduction a week or so before, Russ comprehensively ignored me, choosing instead to move around the farm like he owned it, doing jobs and chores with total autonomy, cleaning the pigs, mucking out the stables and even driving the tractor down to the bottom fields, I wasn't altogether sure what for. But everything he did was performed with a combination of laconic disinterest and consummate ease. But at three years older, he towered above me and was obviously far more knowledgeable about Absolutely Everything and I was just a child. His interest in me however, altered completely in just one day.

I had wandered over to the stables, having already explored pretty much every other area, the pond, the chickens, the pigs, the hay-barn, the vegetable patches and the long greenhouses harbouring among other things, endless, pungent tomatoes. The playroom was all very well, but it wasn't much fun on your own. There was only so long you could spend with the table tennis table half upended, batting against yourself.

Spying a horse that had stuck his head out to see what was occurring in the yard, I went over to see if I could introduce myself. He seemed amenable to my slow, respectful though not inapprehensive approach. I mean, he was massive. I very tentatively put a hand out and he let me stroke his veined nose, however, he seemed more interested in whether I had anything for him, shoving and sniffing at my pockets. I immediately cast around for some succulent grass. The heatwave had done a good job of browning nearly all of it, but where the horse-trough leaked behind the manure heap, there remained a small oasis in green.

Reaping a good fistful, I returned, mindful to present it with a flat hand. He gratefully swept it up, his soft lips rolling across my palm, feeling at once both repellent and ticklishly gratifying. I trotted back and made a better go of gathering more grass, careful to leave out the mudded roots this time, noting that he had carefully cropped them off with the first mouthful.

"He's very naughty." I spun round, half guiltily, as a tall girl wearing jodhpurs, boots and a riding hat strode towards me. She was probably about 16 and I was in love. I knew in just that fraction of a second that it takes to twist neck, swivel eyeballs and refocus on a new object that I was completely smitten. If I could have gone and pulled up great, juicy armfuls of grass for her, if it would have made any impact, I would have hand-reaped a field, right then.

"He prefers apples though." She continued, pulling a Bramley from her pocket.

She was right. The horse had already swung his enormous neck, along with all of his attention around on her arrival, craning even further over the stable door. She lavished an affectionate, familiar hand over his snout and neck, planting a kiss on the bridge of his nose, whilst simultaneously offering up the apple, in one smooth, practiced, elegant movement and I decided at that precise instant that it really wouldn't be so bad to be a horse. Well, that horse in particular.

"What's his name?" I'd asked the question before I fully understood if I was able to in the circumstances, but then leant back mentally to see what might happen next, having already taken that leap.

"Jet" she said, patting and leaning her lithe body into him. She had ladybirds crawling through the curls in her hair, but somehow they looked perfect. I felt elated that I had got his gender correct and even more so that she was still speaking to me.

"Jet. Nice name. From the stone… Lignite?"

"Yes, that's right." She smiled.

"That's a good name."

She looked pleased.

"Helen."

"Hi. I'm Ash."

"Oh, yes, you're Laura's grandson, is that right?"

"Yes. I'm staying here…"

"Well, it's a lovely place to stay."

"Yes. Do you want to play table tennis?"

"Oh, no I can't. I have to look after Jet."

"Oh, ok." I said. I immediately started my retreat; the table tennis was without doubt, my very best gambit and I was now fresh out of ideas.

"He needs to be exercised… cooped up in here all night, it's not good for him."

To reinforce the point she kissed him between the eyes again, squishing her nose right into him as she did so. I figured he had to be swishing his tail as she did that, even though it was out of view. I certainly was, just watching.

"I take him down to the bottom fields and onto the bridleway."

"Oh. Ok." I didn't know there was a bridleway. I wasn't even sure I knew what a bridleway might be. It sounded like a road for horses though, so I was surprised there was one down there that I hadn't noticed. I wanted to know everything there was to know about bridleways and that one in particular. Her soft gaze flickered from my face, over the top of my head and back, but her tone changed completely.

"So, I'll see you around then." She said.

"Yeah. See you around."

With that, she opened the stable door and disappeared in. I thought about peering in after her, but at that moment heard a shuffle behind me and turned to find Russ who'd been watching our exchange, I wasn't sure for how long.

"Alright?" He said.

That was the first time he had volunteered any interest in me at all. I realised it was Russ she had been looking at when her demeanour had altered and I searched his face for any clues as to how well they knew each other. They must know each other, after all, Jet was stabled here and he worked here. They must be a similar age too.

"I was just saying hi to Helen." I ventured.

"Yeah." He fell into step next to me as I headed in the general direction of the house. Come to think of it, Jet's was the only stable I had seen him slop out.

"You wanna see something?" He said.

"Ok." But I was guarded. The one and only time we had played together had involved Hamlet, the last time I had stayed. The game involved taking him down to the bottom field and getting him to sit. Hamlet wasn't the greatest at discipline. I had a feeling that he did as he was asked only when it suited him. After all, I reasoned, who was really going to argue with a 6'4" Great Dane? But if it was dinnertime, or if Grandma asked anything of him, he just rolled over. Anyone else took their chances. So, as we walked Hamlet down the fields, going through one gate and then the other, Russ explained the rules. We would get him to sit at the bottom of the bottom field then slowly walk away, making sure he remained sat. Then, when we were over the first gate and at least half way through the second field, we would start running for the barn, needing to clear one more fence and then make it across the yard before we reached the barn and the safety of the hay bale stack.

Hamlet would most likely manage to remain sitting for as long as we remained at walking pace, but the moment we started to run, he would get excited, ignore any instruction and set off in pursuit. I started to ponder where I needed to be before we started to run, to give me the time I needed to get into the hay-barn and up into the bales before he reached us. He was such a huge dog, once at full pace, he could probably cover an entire field in less than 10 bounds. Looking at his length as he walked beside us, I began to feel I would need to be a good way up the second field, if not already over the second fence and in the yard to be assured of safety.

We started the game as planned. Hamlet obediently sat in the field, tongue out to one side as Russ very quietly unhooked the short leash from his enormous studded collar and we started softly edging away, turning around every few paces to reinforce the order for him to 'Sit', to 'Stay', but he was already looking dodgy. He loved nothing more than a good game, but no one ever played with him because he was just so damn' big. You couldn't tussle or wrestle with him, or even try and pull at one end of a stick, because he'd simply toss you across the yard when he pulled back. I understood the phrase 'he doesn't know his own strength' when I first encountered Hamlet. Right now, his ears were pressing forward and he had that look on his face he got when you were opening the cupboard with the Bonio's in it, even when you were nowhere near the Bonio's. I was only half way over the first fence when Russ broke for the barn.

From my wobbly perch I looked back at Baskerhound. He needed no second invitation, launching off the ground like a Surface to Air missile. I shouted 'Stay!' but knew as I said it that the words may as well have been ceramic tiles falling from my mouth. Saliva streaking his cheek, canines bared white; his lips disappeared as he sprinted across the field, each easy stride eating the feet between us. Leaping down, I pegged it as hard as I could, as hard as my legs would carry me. I swear, I have never run harder than I did right then.

Ahead of me, Russ had already hurdled the second gate in a wizard, one-handed, leg-swinging vault. He was a picture in gleeful excitement, screaming at me, exhorting me to 'run', 'run harder', 'run faster', that I could 'make it'. Hamlet must have cleared the first fence like a Grand National stallion, for I wasn't even half way over the second field when I heard the double thud of his fateful footfall right behind me.

I turned, thinking I might be able to reason with him but, at a distance of over ten feet, he was already post-pounce, mid-air, full flight, mouth open, ears pricked, forelegs rolling his immense paws forward for impact, looking for all the world like the proverbial Hound of Hell. I think it may have come out as a scream, but all I was trying to say was 'Hamlet, No' before he smashed full bore into my chest, bowling me over, punching the wind clean out of me.

I sailed backwards through the air, smacking my head as I landed, rolling a sort of twisted full back somersault before coming to rest, but was immediately pinned into the dry, long grass by ten stone of panting, slobbering dog licking my face, forcing his doggy breath and glutinous saliva into my earhole, up my nose and into my mouth, spread-eagled and helpless as I was. It really hurt and I was really scared, unable to breathe under his pinning bulk, but it wasn't his fault. That night, as I got ready for bed, I had discovered a dead grasshopper crushed in between my bum cheeks.

Pinky and Perky were great. There, you really felt more of an interaction than with any of the other farm animals, beyond just the feeding. They liked nothing more than a really good scratch and could lean on you so hard it was difficult to stay standing, if you got it right. It was like you were hypnotising them. I'd heard about tickling trout and figured it must feel like that to the pig. Russ had seen me scratching Perky before and right now, he was leading me over to the pigpen. However, we walked right past and went on down the yard a way, where he stopped at an ancient, red plastic kids slide nestling in nettles by the top fence.

Although I had no idea what we were up to, so far I couldn't see any foreseeable injury to my person, so elected to play along until I could perceive a reason not to. We went to pick it up, although I had no idea what we were doing with it, but somewhat gingerly avoiding the nettles, I mutely took the light end, manfully struggling with it over to the pigpen. Russ proceeded to heave it over the pig fence and then clambered in after it. I followed suit, even more mystified. We set it up, Russ ensuring that the ladder and frame sunk a fair bit into the mud, less steep than it was designed to be, but we made sure it was stable and upright and Russ humped a hay bale down at the back end.

There being a hosepipe ban, he then doused it in several bucket-loads of water from the butt, making it really wet, the mud at the bottom almost knee deep and then rubbed slippery mud down the slide too. I couldn't see how we were going to use it now, especially after my stair-slide debacle and I really didn't think Gran would thank me for caking all my clothes in clay so thick I could be baked, however much fun it might be, but he ushered me out of the pen and we stood back and watched.

To my amazement, Perky headed straight for the ladder at the back and, using the bale, clambered up onto the top of the slide, then simply crouched and slid himself down it on his belly. I screamed with laughter. At first, I thought he must have done it by mistake... as though he had climbed up through curiosity and then sort-of lost his footing, but he hit the mud, grunting in a really soft, pleased way and headed straight back to the bale to do it again. I think Russ enjoyed my reaction more than how funny it was watching Perky and I guessed he must have done this many times before. Perky was priceless, but Pinky was next to us, sitting back watching him, totally bemused, like Perky must be a complete idiot, which just served to make it all somehow that much funnier.

Russ turned out to be demon at table tennis, smashing me all around the room. He also knew all the lyrics to Queen, and Bowie, although he didn't much go for Supertramp. It was interesting, when the music was playing and he knew we were unobserved, he would fool around, jumping on the sofa playing guitar and singing Freddie Mercury at the top of his lungs. He was completely different to the boy I knew out on the farm. But I'd had some experience of that duality before. It wasn't the first time I'd had friendships that were one way with me when we were on our own and then completely different when anyone else was witness.

He was also a mine of information, not only on bands, but all the telly programs I was missing -Hong Kong Phooey, Wacky Races, Vision On, Top Of The

Pops, Blue Peter, Animal Magic, Swap Shop and Crackerjack. I chose to keep quiet about Play School, Jackanory and The Clangers.

The following day, Russ asked me if I could drive. I weighed up the chances of a lie working, but figured it was easy for him to sit me on the Massey Ferguson and find me out, so admitted that I couldn't. He marched out of the playroom in a manner demanding to be followed and we made our way out past the barns and chickens, heading down towards the bottom field. I'd noticed on previous excursions that there was a very sorry looking matt-grey minivan down there, lying semi-derelict in the overgrowth, several panels and a bonnet missing. He didn't bother opening the door, but slithered expertly into the passenger seat through the missing window. There was no need for me to follow suit, as the entire driver's door was in fact also missing.

Once sunk into the extremely low seat, he proceeded to talk me through the rudiments of driving. The wheel was obvious and I knew that one needed to brake and change gear, but hadn't really considered the actual mechanics of it all before. He patiently walked me through it all until I felt I had a handle on it, then he got out, sending me round to the passenger seat. He fiddled with the engine for a moment, then sat in the driver's side and, to my astonishment, after a couple of tries, started it up. For some reason it hadn't occurred to me that this car actually worked or indeed, that a car without a bonnet or a door could work, for that matter.

But, once he'd added a plank to the seat, raising me up enough to look over the dash, we proceeded to motor around in grassy circles, Russ shouting advice and instruction over the engine noise, made substantially louder by the missing bonnet, dodgy exhaust and lack of a door. I watched intently and then, transferring the plank, took my turn in the driver's seat. My first and indeed second act was simply to stall the engine but, after a couple more goes and a lot of encouragement, I was soon traversing around in slow, deliberate circles on the newly flattened track, even threatening to change into second gear.

When we eventually stopped, I saw I had had an audience. Helen was sitting on Jet at the top of the field watching, whilst Jet contented himself with the long grass growing under the fence. By the time I got there however, she had disappeared, presumably back to the stables and I felt inhibited from going there when in the company of Russ. I felt there was an unspoken understanding. I couldn't think what he must have done to her to make her dislike him so. After his initial indifference, he really had been very decent to me, all in all.

Later that day, Gran enlisted my services on a trip into the village to drop off some veggies, collect a mended saddle and buy some fuses and lightbulbs. I was eager to go, as much to observe how driving was done on a real road, as the prospect of a Curly Wurly and studied both Gran and the road with a newfound interest borne of knowledge. The clutch/gearstick procedure was of particular interest, especially going into third -and what happened with the gearstick when you stopped. On the way back, we were travelling at some speed along a straight section of country road, my attention on the speedo, when Gran braked suddenly and then pulled over, the two wheels under me mounting the grass verge.

"What's happened?" I asked.

"Don't worry." She said. "The car in front just hit a pheasant."

With that, she unbuckled, got out of the car armed with a piece of sacking from the rear seat-well and walked ten yards or so back down the road. I manoeuvred myself to view in the side mirror in time to see her crouch down in the grass. Surely if the pheasant was struck by a car moving at that speed, it was going to be beyond saving. Certainly the offending car hadn't stopped to see if it was alright. Maybe it would be a Police matter, but if it was, I only remembered the car was a red Ford Consul, not the reg.

She returned momentarily with the bird wrapped in the sacking and, timing her re-entry with passing vehicles, duly plonked it on my lap as she sat. I looked down. It looked very dead to me, although it wasn't the expected horrible splatter. It evidently hadn't passed under the tyre, but appeared to have just clipped its head. The rest of the bird looked pretty perfect, with fine, mottled brown markings, spreading warm on my lap. I stroked its feathers as we continued our journey back to the farm; so beautiful. That Sunday, we had pheasant roast.

Chapter VII
1976

Quite what to do with the boy had been a bit of a running dialogue. I was less inclined to be as prescriptive as I know Gillian had been with him, not least because it was his summer holidays. However it was also true that being too idle in this environment for too long might conceivably lead to mischief, there being plenty of mischief to be had on a farm. I kept a covert eye on him, just from time to time, keeping tabs that he was alright and not doing anything to injurious either to himself, or any of the livestock, but it was already apparent to me that the farm, or Kent in general had a far more calming effect on him than the boy we met when on occasion, we went up to town.

From time to time, I would point him towards things, like the fishing rods and tackle, tacitly encouraging him to explore further afield than just the playroom, or indeed the farm, but he didn't bite. He was certainly willing enough to do anything he was asked, like carry vegetables to the house, water plants, or help with painting a gatepost, but I knew this wasn't the answer. In the end, more than likely, it needed to come from him.

It was at that point I struck upon the germ of an idea, more by luck than judgement. One of the useful items I had been forced to re-home from Ash's new bedroom was an old homemade metal detector. Laura had already started to grumble about it, even though it was well out of harm's way behind the bathroom door. As I resolved to take it down to the shed, Ash appeared on the landing.

'Help me take this down to the shed, will you?' Without hesitation, he took it off me and, as we headed downstairs, I resisted an automatic temptation to warn him about the paintwork, as he was already making a good fist of being careful.

"What is it?" He said.

"That? It's an old metal detector. You never know what you might find in these parts. Roman silver, Celtic gold..." I could never resist appealing to the imagination.

"Have you found any?"

"Oh, no. I've not used that thing for many a year. I don't even know if it even works still, you know."

"How do you make it work?"

Bingo.

We went instead to my barn and put it up on the workbench. I was pretty sure with a new battery it would be right as rain, but this appeared an opportunity too good to miss. It was the first discernable thing he'd shown any interest in other than eating, since he'd arrived. As a semi-avid reader, he'd even ignored the books I'd planted, which I thought extraordinary, considering there was no telly. Ash looked wide-eyed around my workshop, formerly restricted access. It was rammed to the rafters with a pretty extensive array of tools across the back wall. Truth be known, I'd been a little chary about sharing this sanctuary with the lad.

"Ok. You need to sand down the handle and shaft, then give it a lick of paint and I'll see what I can do about fixing it. How's that?"

He took the sandpaper without a moment's thought and stood expectantly as I undid the few screws holding it together. He immediately set to work, more enthusiasm than skill but, with a little guidance, soon set about cleaning it up.

I tinkered about with the business end, watching him properly for the first time over my specs. He was bent intently over his task. Maybe there was something after all.

"When you've done sanding, wipe it down with a cloth soaked in turps.' I dropped a cloth on the bench. 'The turps is..."

"I know turps." He said.

It was always hard gauging what was useful and what condescension. So, that was to be my lesson.

The metal detector was basically in good shape and, as first thought, all it needed was a fresh batch of batteries and a clean-up of the corroded terminals. There really isn't much that can go wrong with a simple metal detector.

After he'd given it a coat of black Hammerite, we adjourned to let it dry and, over a lunch chiefly consisting our greenhouse fruit and vegetables, conversation waxed over the finer details of metal detecting... what was its range, what metals it detected, how deep could it sense, etc. The look on Laura's face was worth its weight in any Celtic gold. That is, until I said-

"You know, it's always good keeping hold of these things, you never know when they might come in useful." Some jokes are years in the making.

Ash picked it up and waved it a little precariously around the workshop, headphones on, listening intently to it responding to metallic objects in his vicinity, the beginnings of a pursed smile creeping into the corners of his mouth.

He then made a few experimental passes around the courtyard and garden, finding a few bottle tops, a dessert spoon in the manure pile and some bits and bobs of 1950's farm machinery just under the dirt surface, behind the barn. I then sent him down into the fields, drawing a cordon with my finger as to where our lands ended, where the common lands were and where to avoid.

From the look on his face, he was still half-expecting me to come with him, to chaperone or look after him, show him how it was done, but by the end of our conversation, it had fully dawned on him that he was pretty much free to do as he pleased. He set off, head cocked, intent on the squeal of the detector in his ears.

Laura suspected how deaf I was. I had hearing aids, but they were just so damned conspicuous. Especially when they started whistling. I hated them. I hated what they stood for and managed without them, in the main. Lip reading, knowing pretty much what someone was going to say and body language. A good part of me would have enjoyed this opportunity to bond with the lad, but I couldn't hear a sodding thing in those headphones, nor his rapid mumble with his face turned away from me. Besides. He needed to get out there and spread his wings.

I watched him wend his hesitant way down the field, the path no longer guiding his course, a completely different set of stimuli now dictating the route and speed of his journey. So young. He took for granted so many things I could not.

That's what happened though. Your body slowly, almost imperceptibly, betrayed you until one day something gave way in a big way. Or your pitiful eyesight failed to pick up on the mosquito that, twenty years before, you would have spotted easily across the bedroom and swatted with the dictionary, long before it could puncture your delicate defences and deliver a knockout blow. All your senses gradually shut down and with it, they closed out your horizons, reducing them one by one. Robbing you of the certainty you took so much for granted, having relied on them for so long.

No more foreign holidays for you. No more double cream, no more alcohol, checking you had remembered something and admonishing yourself for having to check, then forgetting the thing that you forgot to check whilst you were occupied over-checking the other thing. The body you no longer recognise coming back at you from the mirror, stubbornly, resolutely no longer doing what you would expect it to do. As if 68 years of servitude was quite enough for any carcass and now it simply 'won't'. As if to underline the withdrawal of services, my sense of taste had abandoned ship along with my hearing. I wasn't yet taking leave of my senses, yet they were surely taking leave of me. I removed my foot from the gate and ambled back to the barn. He'd be just fine. My knees hurt. No sudden moves. I had a dull ache in my gut, which was new.

One of the God-given rules of life must be that you die before your daughter, before your son, if you have one. The ache in my gut was psychosomatic, of that I was certain. Laura had it 10,000 times worse, all her bustle in the kitchen a mask for the amount she was no longer eating. There's nowhere to put it. If I could have cut out Gillian's cancer and eaten it raw, I would have. If I could swap organs with her, I would.

There was nothing I wouldn't give to keep her alive and well and, as I thought this thought, I realised I wouldn't hesitate to do it as much for my wife as my dear daughter girl and it made me weep as I stood there, in the stillness of my workshop. Weep such that I had to hold on to the bench to keep from falling, falling like a stack of dry bones in a museum. A hollow crust of the beast that once roared in this frame.

Am I a god-fearing man? Perhaps half of me, but half of me isn't. The part of me that's Laura is. For many, as one ages, hedge-betting becomes a greater preoccupation, but for me if anything, it becomes less so. I attend church, but only for her. If I lose my darling daughter though, He's lost me forever.

Chapter VIII
1976

I spent two days X-raying the yard, behind the barns and the fields, my best find being a thick, rusty chain. I wasn't sure what it was for though. It was a funny thing in summer. One day, everything's normal and the next, the whole sky is full of flying ants. They were everywhere and would land on any part of you without the faintest sense of wrongdoing, so they would get in your mouth, your hair, your eyes, down your shirt and they just kept coming. Along with the ladybirds, you constantly seemed to have a minor, ongoing insect emergency of one sort or another, throughout the day.

Scanning the heat-hazy landscape through binoculars from the vantage point of my bedroom window, I spied, well beyond the farmland and to one side of the wood, a dip in the ground; potentially a pond that looked to have dried up in the drought. I straightway imagined that someone could well have dropped things in there when it was a pond and that I might find something of value in the mud, like coins, a 9carat gold necklace, or something. At any rate, I figured no one with a metal detector would have been over it already.

Armed with my newly acquired short spade and a flask of tap water Gran passed me, I marched purposefully across the yard, the detector now sporting a leather-belt shoulder strap to aid in the carrying. I waved to Helen as she arrived for Jet and set off down the field, boosted by my decision. Russ was watering the ducks. He'd seemed singularly unimpressed by the metal detector and it occurred to me that he had perhaps already worked over the whole area pretty thoroughly in the past, from the lack of interest on display.

I passed with difficulty through the gate at the bottom of the field, onto the track I now realised was the bridleway Helen had mentioned and circled the woods, avoiding the deep, rock-hard hoof prints made an aeon ago in wetter times. After a couple of wrong turns and much entanglement between foliage and equipment, I negotiated the route down to the pond I had spotted so astutely from afar. Sure enough, flanked by dried bulrushes, there was indeed a banked dip in the ground, smooth mud cracked into uneven, haphazard paving tiles, with clumps of dried weed all that betrayed the existence of water, save a darker, distinctly muddy patch right in the middle. I started by picking my way around the edges, among the reed beds, reasoning that if I was a girl sporting a gold bracelet, this would be where I might drop it.

My early finds numbered yet more bottle tops, a saucepan handle, a paint can and some rusty metal spikes. Losing a little of my earlier optimism, I moved towards the deeper end. Then I hit, the detector registering something quite sizeable and definite under my feet. I stopped for a moment and thought. I really didn't need to be digging up a cast iron sewage pipe, or the like. It was too hot to be doing anything stupid. But then, I figured there wouldn't be a sewage pipe going into or out of this pond, mainly because we were a long way from any houses. I looked around again. There appeared to be no building works of any kind, like drainage, or a sluice, or anything. No tell-tale brickwork. I wasn't entirely sure what a sluice was, but I knew they existed around canals and lakes and besides, I liked the word, sluice.

The signal seemed to clearly indicate that it was just an isolated thing, with no other connection in any direction, so unlikely then to be an underground pipe of any kind. It could be gold... thrown into the pond to hide it. Or buried there, before it even was a pond. Gold didn't rust, so it could have been there a long time and, judging by the undisturbed nature of the surrounds, whatever it was had indeed been there a long time. I pulled off the detector and, retrieving my spade, started to dig, satisfied with my extensive reasoning.

The soil proved to be relatively heavy clay and although the surface was dry and crisp, underneath proved still quite moist, making heavy work. Digging down a couple of feet revealed nothing at all and I clambered out of my hole to take a grateful swig of water and again verify the signal was still there on the detector. It was indeed still there and even more definite, if anything. Ignoring the flies as best I could, I set about it.

"What have you found?" Said a voice.

I looked up to see Helen atop Jet on the bridleway.

"I'm not too sure. It seems quite big though." I replied.

"Ooh. Exciting. Maybe it's buried treasure." She said. Jet didn't look quite so convinced, his attentions directed further up the path, his tail taking care of the flies circling his pampered rump.

"It's a long way down." I said, digging with a renewed effort, in a very professional way, under her interested gaze.

"I shall be back in a while to find out."

"Rightio." I said, heaving another massive slice of clay from my quarry.

"I think I've eaten half a pound of insects just getting this far." She said.

"You need a visor." I said. She smiled, her attention now on persuading Jet to stop eating and presently cantered off up the bridleway, mouth pursed, batting more insects from her face as she went. I looked down again. I should have said mask. 'You need a mask', not a visor. A fly could get behind a visor. I was knackered and I had things crawling all over me I couldn't be bothered to sort out. It was a losing battle out here. There was no sign yet of whatever it was. It could be buried treasure, though. Either it was dropped overboard and sank into the mud, or someone had indeed come in here and actually buried it.

I suspected the latter, because it really was a long way down. Anyway, who would put a big boat on this small pond? My spade eventually clanked against something, so I knelt down and scrabbled with my fingers for a better look. Whatever it was it was hard. Metallic and… black. That ruled out gold and silver. It was really solid though and big. I couldn't locate an edge and went back to using the spade. Whatever it was, it really was pretty substantial. I eventually worked out the size of it. It was sitting in the ground at an angle and it was kind of vast. Like a boulder. So maybe it was a meteorite. Digging around it made me no wiser as to what it might be, as the surface seemed too smooth to be a meteorite and it seemed to be no closer to being dislodged from its seat in the clay either.

I sat down for a rest on the rim of my excavation, drinking my lukewarm water, tipping the last of it over my head. I wished I had a hose that I could at least stick my head under, then also clean the mystery lump up a little and try to work out what I had, but no hose was going to reach here, with or without a hosepipe ban. Whatever it was though, I knew I was going to need help. I wondered whether Jet could be persuaded to pull on a rope. You really wanted a Shire though. I looked up the path to see if there was any sign of her return. She looked good on a horse. Sort of like she should be there.

I went back and rubbed the corner I had first exposed. What on earth was it? Where the spade had hit, black paint had come away to reveal grey metal beneath... definitely manmade. A cold hand clutched my heart when I thought it indeed might just be a pump for the pond. I got up and had another good look at the pond area. It certainly wasn't big enough to be described as a lake. It was a pond. No, I was 60% sure it wasn't a pumping mechanism, after all, there was no vent, or entrance to a pipe anywhere to be found. So the main problem still remained; how was I going to get it out? Whatever it was. Even if I had managed to dislodge it enough to move, it was already pretty clear it was going to be too heavy to lift.

The sound of hooves and a derisory horse snort raised me from my contemplation.

"What is it? Anything?"

"I'm not sure. It's big though, I can't move it."

"You've got something?" She asked, dismounting.

"Yes. It's not gold. Or silver. It's big though." She tied Jet loosely to a fencepost, descended easily and peered carefully into the hole.

"Oh, my. That is big. What is it?"

"Maybe a pump..?" I said.

"It seems a funny thing to be all the way out here. Maybe it's an old tractor." She said.

I hadn't thought of that. That's exactly what it was. A bloody thumping tractor someone had dumped in the pond, thinking no one would ever find it. No one but a prize doughnut like me with a metal detector, that is. What a waste of a day. She must think me a right berk.

"You have to get it out though." She added.

"You think so?"

"Oh, definitely."

"I can't move it. It's massive." I said, looking over at Jet.

"You just need the tractor."

Of course. The tractor! Why didn't I think of that? That's exactly what I needed. Russ and the tractor. I looked at the flies congregating on the damp earth I had excavated and wondered whether, by him using the tractor, it affected my finders' keepers' rights- if he was the one to actually pull it out of the ground.

"I'm going back up. Do you want me to send Russ down?"

"Yes, that would be.... yes, thank you." She looked around the arid pond.

"Poor fish. Well done you, though. Good idea looking here, no one would think of looking in here, would they?" she said. Her praise outshone the sun.

Ten minutes later, I heard the tractor making its way down the field, pausing at the gate and then out along the bridleway. It was no wonder I hadn't spotted the bridleway before, as Jet seemed to be the only horse that actually used it, even though there were countless hoof-prints cast in the hardened mud.

Russ pulled up and jumped down to have a look. He cast a trained eye over the hole in general, the pond, the approach to the pond from the bridleway and finally, on the object itself, in a way that suggested he was weighing up how best to attach a rope to it. In all this time, he didn't say a word. Not a 'what is it?' or an 'Oh, that's a hoojamaflip', or even 'wizard.' I left it as long as I could.

"What do you think?" I figured that was an open enough question that any answer he gave would afford me something, whether he chose to take it to mean 'what do you think it is?' or 'what are our chances of getting it out?' Either way was good.

"We need to dig down at least 'til we can get around it." He paused and then nodded as he left. "We'll need a sling and the barrow."

Meaning I was the one to be doing the digging. Well, if that secured my finders' keepers' ownership, I was ok with that. I recommenced excavations, as Russ headed back to the farm. By the time he got back, I'd made good headway, directing my efforts into creating a clear channel around my quarry. Between us we fed the sling around its middle with a slipknot and then Russ attached that to a rope on the towbar of the tractor. I didn't ask whether it might be a pump for the pond, as I figured he would already have said something to that effect by now and not be as resolved in pulling it out of the ground as he evidently was. Helen reappeared, on foot this time and watched from a safe vantage point, very much out of the way of proceedings.

I climbed out of the hole, standing clear as Russ remounted the tractor, revving it and slowly taking up the slack of the rope, leaning back and twisted around in the seat to watch how the sling was doing. It bit into the edge of the hole I'd dug and Russ smeared some more pedal.

The rear tyres dug into the concrete mud on the bank for purchase and an angry plume of smoke pushed up into the sky, as the tractor applied itself more seriously to the task. But just as he started, he stopped. Taking a water bottle from the tractor, he jumped down again, emptying the contents around the circumference of my mystery treasure. The water pooled, rather than soaking immediately into the ground. It really was very claggy. Seemingly content with this, Russ again jumped up on the tractor and gave it a pull in earnest.

"It's moving!" I cried, above the bellow of the tractor engine. Sure enough, the tractor inched forwards and then lurched, as the lump loosed its earthly bonds, the clay finally relinquishing its hold with a sucking, squelching noise. Helen jumped excited, clapping her hands. It looked like it could be an engine of some description, perhaps she was right. As soon as it was clear of the hole, Russ stopped, slackened the rope, slid the barrow under it and re-attached it with a firmer hold to drag it clear and into the rear barrow.

This done, I gathered my bits and pieces and we headed on back up to the farm, my muddy new acquisition strapped securely into the barrow at back of the tractor, me with Helen, walking along behind.

Once back in the yard, Russ and I sloshed it liberally with buckets in an attempt to wash the worst of the dirt off, but it wasn't cleaning easily, the clay proving pretty waterproof. It was a relief to feel the cool of the water on my arms and I realised how spent I was. After all my exertions, I didn't feel at all elated at the size of my find. Helen again stood back and I sensed a real reticence on her part to get involved with anything that Russ was doing, at least directly, although he didn't seem to care one way or the other.

"What have you got there?" Said Grandad from the door of the workshop. After a moment, as no one else was offering I said

"Helen thought it might be a tractor engine." He approached and bent over the glistening, muddy chunk, running his fingers lightly over the misshapen lump, finally poking it in the ribs.

"No…" He said, pulling a rag from his back pocket.

"Not a tractor?" Not even a tractor, what else was there? Some old banger? Maybe it was a big end. I didn't know what a big end was, but it looked like it was big enough to be one. What a waste of time. Most of all, I wished with all my heart that Helen hadn't been here to witness it all.

"Come and have a look at this." Said Grandad.

His tone made us all gravitate. Russ and I went over and peered into the hole he'd made in the midriff. The clay was still smeared, but there appeared a brass plate, which he'd successfully wiped almost clear. Upside-down, the plaque clearly said '…PRIMED WITH ONE PINT OF OIL THROUGH BREATHER CONNECTION WHEN MOTOR IS REMOVED…' Grandad remained bent, motionless for a moment, not even looking at the plate any more, but at the ground where the water had darkened the dust, however, he seemed genuinely moved by the find. There was more to the plate and I enthusiastically rubbed the rest clean.

"STARTER GEAR MUST BE PRIMED WITH ONE PINT OF OIL THROUGH BREATHER CONNECTION WHEN MOTOR IS REMOVED…"

"-And replaced," finished Grandad.

"…AND REPLACED." I confirmed. "How did you know?" He stood up slowly and stared at me with the funniest serious look. He almost looked to be in pain.

"Do you know what you've found?" I shook my head, quite worried now.

"A Merlin." He said.

I carried on looking at him, right into the black dots centring the grey of his eyes. I knew what a Merlin was. It just didn't make any sense.

"That's a Merlin?"

"That's a Merlin. Where did you find it?"

"In Baggett's Pond" said Russ. "It's all dry as a bone."

Grandad bent down and held my face.

"Do you know what a Merlin is?"

"Engines from the Second World War. Used to power Lancaster bombers and Spitfires." I replied, very quickly.

"And Hurricanes." said Russ.

"…And Hurricanes. Rolls Royce." I added, but that really was all I had.

"Well done. Yes. Rolls Royce, indeed." He turned back to the engine.

"Fabulous!" Said Helen.

"Fabulous." He agreed. And I really think he meant it. "In Baggett's Pond. Well I never."

I was elated.

"Yes!" I jumped around, more relieved than anything. How fantastic. And then I stopped as quickly as I started and spun around.

"Do you think it's a Spitfire engine?" I asked. Everything hinged on this. Everything.

"Very possibly, yes, I do." He beamed.

Oh, joy unbounded. I shook my fists at the sky and danced around like I'd scored for England, leaping in the air in a small circle, waving my arms about, making so much noise even Hamlet came out to see what all the commotion was about. This was amazing. A.mazing. To think; I had unearthed the Emperor of all Engines- of all time, anywhere in the world. I was probably even a millionaire, right now; it must be worth millions, a Spitfire engine. Just wait 'til I told my Mum. 'Til I told all my mates... the Deputy Head Mistress. They'd see just who I was. Who they were messing with. Oh, boy. The jackpot and I was the King. I was the best boy ever to swing a metal detector. I was A Genius. I'd be in The Beano. Maybe even get on Top of The Pops and meet David Bowie and we'd travel through Space together in a tin can. Even Russ looked impressed.

Chapter IX
1941

There was a puff of smoke out of my port window and instinctively I'd pulled away. I had erred over a train yard that evidently had a battery. There was a huge, jarring bang, lifting and throwing us sideways, followed momentarily by another. For a second, I couldn't work out quite what had happened. Evidently hit, I didn't understand why we were still in the air. A quick scan of the instruments as I righted myself, as much as the aircraft- still confusion. Looking once more out of the window, I now saw a gaping hole unnervingly close to me in the port wing, ruptured upwards, but no smoke. No flames.

My eyes again examined the instrument panel, but we appeared to be surprisingly unscathed, apart from the obvious. For one crazy moment I conjectured that I was in fact dead, I just hadn't realised it and I just thought I was still flying, rather like a chicken with its head cut off. It only lasted a fraction of a second, but even as I was thinking this, my brain was also sending messages to the four corners of my body and coming back with irrefutable confirmation that I was indeed alive and well, if a little shell-shocked. And all this time, I was still staring a little distractedly down at the gap in my wing, replaying the moment in my mind's eye and could only conclude that the shell must infact have passed straight through the port wing frame without detonating, only to explode momentarily thereafter, just above and behind me as I travelled forwards. Suddenly claustrophobic, I pulled my mask off as I pondered the miracle.

If I had been in a Hurricane, by hitting the wing, the shell would have passed straight through the fuel tank, which would have done for us. Not only because of the resultant explosion, the loss of fuel, the undoubted loss of wing, but also because the wing roots of a Hurricane pass hollow and open, straight into the cabin. Any fumes or flames in the wings would therefore surge unfettered directly into the cockpit, giving me next to no time to react, neither to land, nor even bail out.

This being a darling Shrew, I had none of these concerns, both my fuel tanks wedged directly ahead of me, protected with bulletproof steel. I had only a yawning hole, increased drag, a strong yawing effect, reduced lift and, now I thought about it, the strong possibility of the loss of the port flaps. Pressingly, what I needed to do now was find a little height, orientate myself more precisely and high tail it back across the oggin to Blighty's welcoming white cliffs. I could worry about landing later.

The channel seemed to take forever to appear and I occupied my time craning my neck and studying the rear view than looking forward, obsessive for possible bandits I was in absolutely no position to do anything about, should any appear. My fuel was low, but sufficient to make it back to base if I avoided any further mishaps, although I'd happily have settled for any base on the other side of the channel.

Right then, I felt very tired. The sweat I hadn't previously been aware I had leaked, reverted frosty on my skin and I took a moment to shake my shoulders and squirm the small of my back, both of which had been locked in the same position for quite some time. One was only in the air for maximum 90-minutes and then she would be all but out of fuel, however, missions sometimes seemed to take an

eternity, far longer than 90-minutes. One all to brief
buddy Benj used to joke that he understood what it
was to be a cat, for he used up an entire life every
time he went up and engaged with the enemy.

Looking back, my sorties all seemed to merge into
one long one, punctuated only by kills, a weekend's
leave spent on the seafront in Westcliffe-on-Sea and
the kisses of Anne, the barmaid in my old local, sadly
no longer my local, when I relocated to the 611 in
Hornchurch. The rest of it, the waiting, the cards, the
food, the take offs, the landings and everything in
between, be it naked fear or cold clinical execution, it
all just rolled into one blurred, homogenous lump.
Where I came from, there was nothing the local girls
liked more than a flyboy. And a flyboy that flew
internationally? Well, then they'd hit the jackpot. But
not over here. I was tired.

As the coast of France at last gave way beneath
me, keeping low enough not to give their defences
any chance to react to my arrival, my eyes
automatically bent on the white cliffs ahead. I
couldn't afford to relax, but they really were a sight
for sore eyes. Pulling on my mask, I forced myself to
focus on what I faced. I had to assume that my flaps
were out. Although I couldn't fathom why, I didn't
feel I even wanted to find out; I was just going to
assume they were. That being the case, I couldn't
afford to engage them upon my approach at low
altitude and have them fail, in any way, shape, or
form. That meant a long landing, without flaps to act
as an airbrake, using the whole of the awfully short
Hornchurch runway, possibly ending up with an
overshoot and an embarrassing muddle in the potato
field at the far end. I still fancied that as an option

over a crash-landing, sideways-on to the direction of travel, or tilted wildly to one side, wingtip diving seconds before touchdown and a cartwheel finale.

As expected, coming in to land was a pretty fraught affair, arriving crabwise as I did anyway due to crosswind, then bouncing about like a pasty-faced novice, not by any means in control of things. I'd never live it down. There had been a nagging concern at the back of my mind that, aside from the flaps, my landing gear might not descend, having also been damaged by the impact, but the increased drag and looked-for green light on approach assured me that all was well down-under and, bolstered by a calm, measured response from base on the headset regarding my impending arrival, I set her as best I could for a three point landing, albeit somewhat askew on direction.

Although I had expected to do so, we hit the ground with a bone-jarring jolt, far faster than even I was prepared for. At this speed, I would ordinarily have recommended a pilot simply abort, throttle up and take off again, however, I didn't have that luxury. We fairly raced across the grass, bumping and bouncing, as I prayed for the tail to hit and thereby increase the drag, slowing us down. The nose finally came up, blocking my forward view, which did nothing to calm my nerves as I belted across acres of turf, engine killed. I started a very slight turn, wondering whether I would be able to fashion a slight 'S' across the field, craning sideways out of the cockpit to try and judge the remaining distance to a relentlessly approaching hedge. Jaw set, arms braced for the inevitable collision, I did however eventually trundle to the prayed for stop, my prop crunching into the dreaded hedge at the other end of the field.

Engaging the stalwart hawthorn as we did had the unexpected effect of lifting the tail of the Shrew off the ground again and, for a moment, just as I had allowed myself to relax from my rigid grimace, dropping my heavy head, breathing out and congratulating myself on saving my own life- whilst bringing a damaged but no doubt eminently repairable aircraft safely back to base- I immediately braced again, believing I was going to suffer the final ignominy of tipping the front-heavy bird on her face, in front of a comprehensive audience of ground crew, staff, pilots, admin and superiors. But we steadied, bobbed, then rested, balanced just so, almost on the horizontal, like a jack-in-the-box coming to rest, to find myself looking over the hedge into the adjoining field, rocking irregularly as if buoyed on a bed-spring, toyed by the gusting wind.

Finally, I let go, making no effort to climb out. The peace and quiet was, I realised, all I needed for the time being, just the sound of the wind and the creak and rustle of branches, punctuated by the metallic tap-tap of cooling exhaust stubs. From my unexpected vantage point, I watched a corbeau, a rook in the bucolic calm of the adjoining field swoop down, performing an impeccable landing and marvelled at how effortless it all was for nature. He didn't even have to think about it, so fluid was the manoeuvre in its execution. Everything I had to torture myself with in my overstrained, over-tired state; the exquisite attention to every detail, the simultaneous factoring of wind-speed and direction, of fuel, landing gear, flaps, airspeed, height, yaw and rate of descent, all of these things were completely instinctive for that impossibly sleek, inimitably engineered gloss-dipped bird.

The sun flashed lightning blue off his immaculate blackness as he stalled with inch-perfection, enabling him gently to extend one foot at almost zero mph and touch down straight into a deliberate, uninterrupted strut over to the object of his attention, without so much as a pause for thought. *Without pausing for thought*. Nothing to ruffle the feathers at all. With neither strain nor effort. His flying-gear collapsing, retracting, with an instantaneous, folding exactness, even as his landing gear touched down, supplying just enough momentum to give his back foot cause to roll forward in unbroken gait. And thus, he sashayed, I felt, with a totally deserving swagger.

I applauded him mentally, as I swayed, ungainly in my kite, perched precariously and somewhat regrettably, rather like a child's toy glider in the neighbour's tree, having demonstrated neither grace nor mastery in my own arrival. He no doubt cast a professional, perfunctory eye over my attempt at landing moments before, full as it was with sound and fury, with a mixture of grave concern (for everything in the vicinity, if not for me), as well as that particular strain of Unbridled Amusement, the sole preserve of 'Those That Can' when looking down upon 'Those That Never Will'. I concluded that, for all of man's superlative brilliance, we didn't hold a candle to Mother Nature, none of us. Idiots indeed.

Brought up a Hindu, I never saw joining the war effort as against my faith. I had come to see that I was less devout than either of my parents, or indeed my brother and sisters. But here, so very many miles from home, there somehow seemed to be less room for religion than ever. Unlike so many of those around me worshipping a Christian God, any connection with something so personal, so intimate as faith just increased the potential for pain to flood in.

Jack slamming my canopy back started me from my meditations and I felt foolish against the weight of concern etched all over his face, unsure of the sight that might greet him. It was clearly evident that he thought I must be at the very least injured, or more likely dead as, usually, I would waste no time escaping my captivity. By rights, I should have hauled the canopy back myself before coming in to land. Ground crew and pilots alike had raced out to meet me and I imagined I must have been one of the last to return. Somewhat selfishly, I hadn't previously thought of them; how it must be to think you had lost a fighter and thus by extension, your pilot and the relief you might feel to see your aircraft appearing one by one over the hedge to touch down moments later, on the green grass of my adopted home.

It was only after I had cadged a lift back, reported my non-tally to the hut, returned to my digs, pulled sodden clothes off a body I no longer recognised and sunk into a steaming bath behind closed door that I started to shake uncontrollably. Two hadn't made it back.

Chapter X

1976

Lunch was spent poring over books of engine diagrams, as Grandad explained in more detail what he thought it might be. His leaning was towards a MkV or something later, owing to the big lump at the back which was the 'Supercharger'. I was ravenous after my morning's exertions, but drank it all in. It really was turning out to be quite fabulous, as Helen said. Better than any treasure. Beyond my wildest dreams.

Russ and Helen had joined us, although Helen contented herself talking quietly to Grandma at the other end of the table about the cost of horse-feed and whether she needed to get one of Jet's hooves seen to. But from Russ's attentions, he was pretty interested to learn from Grandad too. After all, how often did you haul a Merlin out of the ground?

That afternoon, I looked on as they wrestled it into Grandad's workshop and then set to work giving it a thorough cleaning. It still had a small section of cowling wrapped around it, which Grandad carefully removed, then I carried on cleaning up. He noted that it was odd that there was nothing else of the aeroplane, just the engine, but to me that was the most important bit. My next find was even more exciting than the first label. It said 'ROLLS ROYCE LTD ENGLAND' then underneath, 'MERLIN No.' and underneath that, 'LIMITATIONS'.

From his various umm's and ahh's, Grandad was very happy with that discovery and retreated again to locate and scrutinise a book. He came back and stopped me.

"Do you want to know precisely what it is?"

"Yes."

"Look, it says here, you uncovered it." He ran his finger over the new plate.

"It's a Spitfire MkV engine."

"Yes! It's definitely a Spitfire?" I hadn't dared presume, but in the intervening time, I had hoped, I had wished so much, so fervently. But it was like winning the Pools and I jumped around all over again, unable to contain it, until he stopped me with a hand on my shoulder, mindful of the fact we were now in a workshop. Grandad then showed me his irrefutable proof. He'd checked the number on the plate against his book and it was, without doubt, a Spitfire. He felt sure we would be able to find out more about it, too.

"Can we fix it?" I asked.

This stopped him in his tracks and he thought for a long moment, looking at me, then away over my head, then back at me.

"There's no harm in trying, is there?" He said.

I didn't remember ever being so excited than at that moment. Not leaping about excited, just quietly, hotly, in my belly excited. Imagine having a working Spitfire engine. How brilliant would that be?

Helen came over from the kitchen to view our progress before leaving. I explained what we knew as I continued to reveal more of the engine with cleaning, basically repeating everything that Grandad had told me in the previous hour. 'It really was in excellent condition, considering it had been buried so long'. 'It was a Spitfire MkV Rolls Royce engine and we knew this because I had discovered the engine badge that numbered the engine precisely'. 'It most likely went into the ground shot down, or crashed, during 1941. At this point she grew a frown and, sensing something was amiss, I tapered off. She turned to Grandad.

"Do you think he died?"

"Well, at the moment, it's impossible to know. They did have parachutes though," he said. "But we can find out for sure. We can even cross reference our records with the German ones, to be sure."

I carried on cleaning. I hadn't even thought about the pilot. I hoped he got out alive.

"I will say though, that there is no evidence of the rest of the aeroplane, just the engine, so who knows what happened." He continued.

She nodded at this, seemingly content for now, then left shortly after and we carried on, a little more subdued than before.

It became evident that the engine was pretty badly damaged by the impact, on the back end in particular, although what there was was in excellent nick, most likely due to the fact that it had gone into a pond; buried in clay, it hadn't been exposed to air, which would have been a killer in terms of corrosion. It was indeed also very curious that there wasn't any more of the aircraft, very little of the outer skin of the aeroplane, certainly no fuselage or wings and only the busted hub of a propeller.

Russ and I went back and made extensive searches of my original site, as well as the land nearby, but discovered nothing further of the aeroplane. Grandad seemed to think that this indicated that the aircraft had possibly broken up in the air, as opposed to hitting the ground whole, making it even more unlikely that the pilot had gone into the same hole as the engine, if indeed he'd died at all. This felt like good news all round. At least I hadn't unwittingly been enthusiastically excavating a grave. Imagine if a bone had turned up. Grandad did make me refill the hole I had made though, to 'leave it just as you found it'.

That evening I cleaned the newly identified 'Merlin 45' up as best I could with soapy water, a floor brush and a dishcloth.

As I stood back admiring my handiwork, Grandad appeared on my shoulder.

"You're quite taken with this, aren't you?" He said. I nodded.

"Is it worth a million, do you think?"

"Well, I wouldn't say that." He said, smiling.

"Not even if it was working? It is rare, right, a Spitfire Merlin engine?"

"Yes, it is quite rare. Although there were more Merlin 45's made than any other Mark."

"Really?" That didn't sound good.

"Yes. But there really aren't very many out there in working order now."

"Oh, ok. So it might be worth something then, right?"

"At the moment, it isn't worth much at all as scrap." He said.

"It's not scrap though. I mean, we can get it working, right? You said it was in good shape, considering…"

He looked at me again. He'd been doing a lot of that.

"Do you really want to clean this up? I mean properly. Like an engineer?" I nodded again, enthusiastically, although I wasn't quite sure what he meant. As far as I could see, it looked pretty good after my latest go at it.

"Right. Well, we'll need to find you some protective clothing and suchlike. Go and ask your Grandmother for some overalls."

I trotted off. It took longer than expected, as there was nothing really small enough. When I came back, Grandad was on the floor, taking the thing apart on a large, folded sheet of heavy plastic and I suddenly realised what he'd meant about cleaning it.

He was very taken by the fact that the engine was, as far as we could ascertain anyway, completely on its own in the pond and, since our discovery, had spent a great deal of time studying various books, drawings and manuals on the subject, even making phone calls, whilst I contented myself with the extensive job of cleaning, piece by piece, until spotless.

I wasn't able to do any of the dismantling, but between them and a good deal of effort, Russ and Grandad got it apart, section by section. There were some bits so badly stuck, it took the best part of a day to loosen them and some bits broke instead of undoing, or needed to be drilled out, which was Grandad's unhappiest choice, but eventually, the engine lay in tidy bits. Hundreds of them, all laid in neat rows. It really was magnificent.

I had no idea there were so many parts to an engine, that they would all fit into that size, or that anyone would have the slightest idea how to put it all back together again. I remembered somewhat shamefully Gran's pride in her husband's profession and my dismissal of him knowing a Spitfire from a Hurricane; straight over my head indeed.

From the damage, Grandad reckoned the Merlin appeared to have gone into the ground in reverse and upside down. This meant that most of the real damage was to the supercharger on the back end, which consisted some of the finer engineering, with a lot of small cogs (or gears, as they were known), pipes and an impellor, which was like a small, internal propeller that pushed the air around. But it was amazing that it had been in the ground for thirty years, it didn't seem like it. I also felt sure that whatever the broken pieces were, with Grandad's knowhow and all the tools in his workshop, we would be able to make replacements. This really was fantastic.

I never realised that cleaning could be such an exacting process, meaning much more than simply rubbing things with a cloth. I also had to wear goggles and rubber gloves much of the time, which got very hot and uncomfortable. As the engine came apart, I would soak the components overnight in tin trays of pungent cleaning fluids, scraping off endless gunge with the end of a screwdriver, a wire brush and even an old toothbrush. I also had to label everything according to the drawings that Grandad produced, which was a long process of creating a wire tag for everything. He was impressed that I knew that 'BS308' was the engineering standard for drawings.

It was all going to be worth it, if we could only put it all back together and get it working. From time to time he would lean over and inspect my efforts. Even Russ, in between farm-work, would come in and lend a hand and we would crouch there, for hours on end, him in a leather farrier's pinny and me in some altered dungarees, scrubbing a gear wheel with a washing up brush, wearing a pair of grimy Marigold's.

At one point, when Grandad was out of earshot, Russ did say he was surprised that I would be at all interested in the War, 'me being Indian 'n all'. I retorted that 'two million Indians died in the War helping the British' and anyway, 'I wasn't Indian, I was English'. He found this mildly funny, but he didn't bring it up again. I realised it was the Deputy Head Mistress who had taught me that in school, but he didn't need to know that.

As the engine came apart it did so in very clear sections and I familiarised myself with the various bits. I wasn't at all sure how it all worked, but I was able to tell my rocker from my piston and know what a sump was for. Funny word though, 'sump'. Russ would name things as he handed them over for cleaning and I would repeat the word and look at the item very closely, committing them to memory as best I could. However, some bits were smashed beyond redemption, so Grandad would have me red-label them and place them in the relevant section, so we knew we needed to find a replacement.

Most things were wildly different, so it was easy to tell them apart, but a few things were harder. There were twelve cylinders to the engine, so that meant quite a few of the components were repeated twelve times, or even more, like the inlet and exhaust valves, where there were two per cylinder, making 24 altogether. I also took to sitting up late, avidly reading up about Spitfires and Merlin engines in particular. Grandad had an endless supply of manuals. It turned out there were two distinct types of engineer, those that worked on the 'airframe', meaning the fuselage, the wings and such like and the Engine technicians. Grandad was Engine. I wanted to be Engine.

The Mark Five Spitfire was introduced in 1941, just after the Battle of Britain, which only lasted three months. I had always thought the Battle of Britain was the whole war in the air, from 1939 to '45, but it was just this short amount of time when Hitler thought he would invade Britain by first gaining air superiority in the summer, between July and September of 1940.

That was where he failed though, losing double the number of aircraft, whilst neglecting to take out important strategic targets, like our early warning system and radar. The Germans also kept changing their focus, from attacking the fighters and their aerodromes, to bombing cities, allowing the RAF enough respite to bounce back, just when they were on the brink of disaster.

Shortly after that, in the September of 1940, Adolf figured it was all too expensive and difficult, so turned his focus and resources on Russia. Another very interesting fact was that because the Spitfires were not designed necessarily with mass production in mind, they were made piecemeal, all across the country. This actually made it very difficult to bomb Spitfire factories, as components were crafted all over the place, whereas prior to the war, the Bosch had studied American car production lines, with the intention of replicating that efficiency with their own plants. At the height of production in Germany, they could turn out a staggering 2,500 Messerschmitts a month, whereas we were managing just 350 Spitfires in the same timeframe, due to the cottage industry method we employed. However, their huge, centralised factories also made glaring targets, as they were so easy to spot and, with everything going on under the same roof, it proved a great deal simpler for us to disrupt their aircraft manufacture in comparison. So interesting.

The Merlin 45 used in the MkV Spitfire was an improvement on the previous engines because of the big, new supercharger, meaning the plane was quicker, could gain height faster from a standing start and could also fly at a higher 'ceiling'. They were also able to put the new engine into older airframes. So a MkII Spitfire became a MkV simply by having a Merlin 45 engine put in, in place of the old MkVII engine it previously contained. Amazing.

So, what I was now the proud owner of, (I didn't believe Russ was making any kind of a claim to it) was a Merlin 45 Rolls Royce engine that went into service sometime in early 1941. I was more and more curious about what had happened to have it end up in Baggett's Pond and what had happened to the pilot, if only to put Helen's mind at rest. Grandad said there was no sign of any shrapnel in the engine, but that was still pretty inconclusive. I had to agree. I mean, maybe the pilot got shot, or the wing was blown off or something. You just wouldn't know from the engine then, would you? Like examining someone's skeleton skull when they've been shot in the heart. Stupid. And Grandad knew everything there was to know when it came to Spitfires.

Mum had been really impressed with my find and told me she wanted to be kept updated. She asked that I write to her, but I much preferred chatting on the phone, cos for one, you could get your words out faster. Somehow she seemed to know a fair amount about what was going on so, often, when I did speak to her, she would ask me questions about things I didn't know she knew. She also sent more clothes down for me, because she wasn't sure when we might get to see each other. Mostly, she wanted to know that I was happy down in Kent.

I got more and more excited about the prospect of getting the engine to work and was impatient to see the commencement of putting it back together, but Grandad seemed to be dragging his feet for no apparent reason, as far as I could see. I decided I would drop a few careful hints over dinner.

"When are we going to start putting it all back together?" I asked, as we pulled in our chairs. Grandma exchanged a look with Grandad and dished up the cabbage.

"Ash, I'm not entirely sure it will all go back together..."

"What do you mean? I labelled everything..."

"...In any kind of working order. What I mean to say is, it's pretty much broken beyond repair."

"But we can fix it. You can fix it. That's what you used to do in the war, that's what you said."

I could feel a lump surging up inside my throat out of nowhere and needed to get all the words out before it stopped me from speaking.

"If we had all the missing parts, all the damaged parts, perhaps we could fix it, but that aeroplane went into the ground at anything up to 600mph, maybe even faster and it's over 35 years old."

"Yes, I know but..." He wasn't finished- "And many of the crucial components are corroded. The air gets to them and the oil. Some parts are magnesium and they just... rot over time."

"But you have the workshop. You have all your tools and machines. We can just make the pieces we need."

"No, Ash, we can't..."

"Why not? Why can't we?" I could feel a kind of panic fighting to get out of my chest and it just made my voice go higher, but this was important.

"We can use the old, broken parts to make new ones."

"There are laws, Ash. You aren't *allowed* to make engine components. That's the law. Take some cauliflower."

"Why is it the law?" I said, doing as I was told.

"Because then any Tom, Dick or Harry might go out there and try to build an aeroplane and then they would start dropping out of the skies like flies. Everything needs to be made from aircraft grade materials and to a very high spec. Aircraft grade metals... and everything needs to be tested and made safe, again to a certain standard. Besides, Rolls Royce has never released and never will release the drawings we would need to make these components."

That was quite an answer. One that needed some time to think about. It was against the law to make engine components. My head sank down and I stared at the blue leaf pattern on my plate. Big, hot tears welled up and started dropping onto my steaming cauliflower. I hated cauliflower. I'd come all this far. He must have known he wasn't going to be able to fix it. He just let me clean it all just to make fun of me.

"Oh, Ted." Said Grandma. "Now look what you've done."

"You're just making fun of me." I said, crossing my arms, aware that my bottom lip was sticking out.

"Come now, darling, eat up before it gets cold." Said Grandma.

"Make me." There was no way they could get my arms uncrossed. They were wrapped so tightly, they could have picked me up by my elbows, but my arms were staying crossed. I knew that for a fact.

"Don't speak to your grandmother like that. Say sorry."

I didn't move. After a moment, Grandad stood up. I shrunk a little further into my chair. He was a big man.

"Come with me." He said. At no point during all of this had he raised his voice. I would never have spoken to my mother like this, I didn't know what had got into me.

"No." I said. "Where are we going?"

"I want to show you something."

I looked at him, mistrustful.

"It's fine. Come."

I looked at Grandma, who offered no resistance to the fact that dinner really would get cold and then slowly slid off my chair. From his vantage point on the floor across the room, Hamlet looked on, concerned. No one ever left a plate of food. Grandad had headed out of the room and was already out of the kitchen door, so I followed at a distance, my arms still very much crossed, as we headed not to the workshop, but to one of the permanently padlocked stables. As we went in, he hit a socket switch and a bare light-bulb on the end of a cable strung loosely up to the ceiling came on.

The space was deceptively large, as several stables had been knocked through to make one cavernous room. There were various objects in the gloom, most under tarpaulin. He went over to one such, up against the wall and beckoned me over. I shuffled forward, definitely intrigued, but still not at all sure if I was going to properly like it. He hauled the tarp off, revealing a rusty metal angle-iron rig, a muscular, shiny black lump suspended within it. I squinted as I moved slowly forward. Even without reading the brass plate, I knew it was a Merlin. A Merlin engine, oil-gleaming black. I couldn't quite believe my eyes.

"Is that a Merlin?" I asked, in spite of myself.

"Yes it is."

I looked at it, my eyes growing more accustomed to the gloom. I couldn't see the familiar supercharger lump on the end.

"It's not a MkV?"

"No. It's a MkXII Merlin, from a MkII Spitfire."

"But…"

"You must promise not to tell your Grandma. Or your mother, alright?"

"I promise. But where did it come from?"

He paused.

"I won it in a raffle."

"You won a Spitfire engine in a raffle?"

"A pub raffle. Well, it was in with a couple of other bits and pieces, but I knew it was a Merlin, so I bought more than half the tickets. Infact, if I recall, this was the Second Prize. The First Prize was a pig and I won that too, which didn't make me very popular, but your grandmother was happy when I came home with a pig. I had to go back and pick up the other pieces, without her noticing, the next day."

"You won a pig and a Merlin engine?" Why didn't I ever get to enter pub raffles? Life was so unfair. "What was the pig's name?"

"Jellicoe. I think I allowed Third Prize, the stuffed goose, to go back into the hat... Anyway, that's neither here nor there. The reason this one has been sitting here forever and a day, is because it's missing several vital components. Components that I thought might come from yours."

I started to feel excitement all over again, casting a professional eye over the MkXII.

"This one looks like the rockers are good..." I offered. "Are they interchangeable though, the MkXII and the 45?"

"The only real difference is the Merlin 45 has the big supercharger on the end, as you know. And, well, it's not complete either, but it's far less damaged and in a different place than your one." He said.

"So, what's wrong with this one?"

"The engine overheated, but it never crashed, it just went as scrap, eventually. See, here." He pointed to one side of the cylinder bank.

"The seals in there failed. They separate the coolant from the engine. If the coolant gets in the engine, then it overheats... So, if we were to..."

"Use the bits from mine and put them together into this one..." I finished his sentence for him, my mind racing at 375mph.

"Or bits from mine to sort out yours..." He said.

"So, we wouldn't need to make *any* pieces, we would just to make one engine from both of them."

"Well, it's certainly worth a try, isn't it?"

"Yes! And we wouldn't be breaking the law." I clapped my hands.

"I also have a couple of trays of bits and bobs from my working days, you know, rather than have them go into a skip, I'd bring them home. I'm still not entirely sure that we will have one complete engine, even at the end of all that though, just to warn you. I wouldn't want any more tears on your cauliflower." He said.

I stared at the black wonder before me. I don't think I'd ever seen anything so beautiful in my life. Apart from Helen, but that was different.

"Now, will you let me go back and eat my dinner?"

"Yes." I said.

"No more tantrums..?"

"No. Sorry."

"That's alright then. Now be sure and apologise to your Grandmother. And don't say anything about this, alright? Do we have a deal?"

"Yes, we have a deal." I said.

We stepped back outside into the courtyard, Jet observing me from his stable door, as if he had known about this MkXII all along and was waiting for me to play catch-up, but I didn't mind, my head was once again in the clouds.

As I watched Grandad lock up I remembered, at school, I had read a poetry anthology and there was one poem... but I couldn't remember anything of it. I hadn't paid it much heed at the time, because Rossi had finally managed to snap his Unbreakable Ruler, but I was pretty sure it was called 'Cathedrals In The Sky' and it was about what it was like to fly up through the clouds during the War. Or maybe it was First World War, even. I couldn't remember. Either way, it had to be the most amazing feeling in the world. It was the reason I think I first got interested in Spitfires.

As we headed back to the house, he dropped a hand around my shoulder.

"I'm sorry I didn't tell you, Ash, but I didn't want to get your hopes up. I didn't want to get *my* hopes up. And we aren't out of the woods yet, by any means."

I looked down. I couldn't remember when my arms became uncrossed, but I was very glad they were.

Chapter XI
1976

The next morning, Mum arrived laden with presents for all of us, but especially me, the main one being a bulky 'The Lord Of The Rings' paperback, by J.R.R. Tolkien. I guess she was feeling guilty 'n all. But I wasted no time in getting her to the workshop and showing her my Merlin. I explained to her all about it and how it was very confusing with the Spitfire Marks and the engine Marks and even how the engine Marks changed over from Roman numerals to English ones around sixteen, when it all got too long in V's, X's and I's.

I wasn't sure how much she took in, but she spent a long time looking at the engine and at me and was very thoughtful. She wanted the whole story from start to finish and we even went down to the pond to see where I found it. On the way, I told her about the pig-slide and learning to drive the mini and pointed out my tree. She wanted to know what my plans were and I told her I wanted to get it working again and eventually build a flying Spitfire.

"Do you really think you can?"

"With Grandad and Russ helping, I don't see why not." I said. She ruffled my hair, which was really annoying, but I let her.

"We'll have to see what they say. It's very different down here isn't it? Do you like it?"

I had to think about this. All Mum's questions weren't just straightforward ones. She was a bit like Grandad in that respect.

"Yes, I like it, but not as much as home." I said.

"But you like it here. You have a lot of things you like here. And the Marlin..."

"It's a *Merlin*, Mum, it's named after a bird of prey, not a fish."

"Merlin, I meant Merlin, yes. Sorry."

"Kestrel, Merlin, Griffon… see?"

"Yes, sorry love."

"And then the bombers were all named after cities. Manchester, Halifax, Lincoln, Lancaster…"

"Right." She said.

She never listened to what I said. I always had to repeat myself endlessly. We stood at the vacant pond, my excavations making a rude mess of the middle, even though I had filled it all in.

"Mum, when do you think I can come home?"

"Well, that was something I wanted to talk to you about. For one, I haven't been able to find a school yet that will take you in."

I had forgotten all about school. It felt like a different world down here. Like the summer would last forever. But of course, that was just ridiculous.

"But I can still come home and be with you, right?"

"Well, honey, I'm still not out of the woods. I'm still undergoing treatment.'

"But I can come and look after you."

"That's not how it works and you know it isn't."

At that moment there was the sound of approaching hooves and Jet passed by, with Helen in the saddle.

"Hi!" she beamed, waving at us.

"Hi." I mustered, flapping my elbow once, hands remaining firmly in pocket.

To my eternal relief, she didn't stop, but headed off up the bridle path and into the woods.

"Ok, who's she?"

"Mum! It's not like that."

"I should say. Did you see how she smiled at you? Ash..."

"Mum!"

"Well, at least tell me her name."

"Helen."

"Hmm. Helen. Helen of Troy. Ash, you Devil."

"Mum, stop it now. You're being really irritating. It's not like that, she's just a friend."

"I always said, with those dark good looks of yours. You're gonna slay 'em. I'm proud of you."

As she said this she ruffled my hair again and this time I pushed her off. She stood for a moment and studied my face as I rearranged my hair.

"You don't hate me, do you love?"

"No, I don't hate you." I said. "Do you hate me?"

"No darling, I don't hate you at all. You're the best thing that ever happened to me. I don't hate you at all." She stopped and frowned at the ground "There were just things... things can be very complicated, you know?"

I looked down too, thinking of all my fire-starting escapades that felt so far behind me right now and felt so ashamed. I wanted to admit to everything there and then and wipe the slate clean.

"Yeah."

"Grandma and Grandad are really proud of you. Nothing but good words. That makes me really very happy, you know? That you're happy down here and things are going well."

Put like that, I suppose I had been very happy.

"Why didn't you tell me about Grandad and the War?"

"What do you mean? I did tell you. You mean about the Spitfires?" I nodded, already less certain.

"I *did* tell you. You just never listen!" She said.

"No, you never. Did you? When?"

"Oh, Ash. I've always told you about the pair of them. Really, sometimes I don't know where your head is at."

"And I don't know where yours is either!" I burst out, stomping back up to the path.

"Oh, Ash. I'm sorry. Please, let's not fight." Stumbling after me, she caught my arm and hugged me.

God. Why was it all so difficult?

"Come on, let's head back. But first I want to see if I can climb your tree."

We went back up to the path and along the side of the woods. It was a perfect summer's day, so still, so hot that nothing was bothering to stir, save the odd insect swinging lazily by. Complete, cotton-wool clouds hung like meringues, motionless in the sky, no wind even up there to move them on.

On a clear day, when I bunked off school, I would go to the playing field and lie spread-eagled on the close-cropped turf to stare up at the sky and, if it was a perfectly cloudless blue day, I would concentrate really hard and make-believe that I was in fact *in* the sky, looking down on the sea, miles below me.

One time I did it and a plane way, way up passed in slow motion overhead, leaving a momentary vapour trail behind and I imagined it was actually a speedboat, scudding across the ocean, far, far below. Just for a few seconds I kidded myself so perfectly that I had to grip tight onto the grass and clench my eyes shut, convincing myself so well that I got vertigo and panicking that I was infact going to fall. Fall out of the sky and drop tens of thousands of feet into the ocean below.

I gave Mum a leg up into the oak and, once she had made herself comfy in my place of habit, climbed past her onto a narrower, less comfortable perch. We sat there in silence for a good long while, just taking in the branches, the tree stretching above us, the smell of the woods, the odd bird twitter and the sunlight shifting gently through the leaves. It was heaven. Mum was right; I did love it here. We heard Helen canter past unseen and Mum couldn't resist reaching up and tugging my foot. I smiled but pretended not to notice.

"It's lovely here, isn't it?" She said.

"Yes, it is."

"Can I tell you a secret?"

"What?"

"I used to climb this very tree when I was a girl."

"You're kidding."

"No, I'm not. This used to be my favourite tree when I was your age."

I realised that this was another statement adding weight to my earlier epiphany; that there had indeed been much Life Before Me. I was still having some trouble wrapping my head around it.

"I haven't spoiled it for you though, have I?" She added, aware of my silence.

"I was just thinking."

"Ok. I would hate to think that you wouldn't come here again, because of me."

I knew what she meant.

"Mum. Are you going to die?" I just blurted it out. I wasn't sure where that came from, but it somehow seemed the right place to ask. As right as anywhere, anyway. It was her turn to go quiet for a while.

"I hope not, darling. I really hope not. But *if* I do, you know that I love you and there are people who will be there to look after you, don't you?"

I didn't want to cry, but I suddenly found myself trying really hard to suppress my sobs, squeezing the branch between my legs and making an effort to slow my breathing, moving really quietly to wipe my tears so that, from underneath, she wouldn't be able to tell.

Chapter XII
1976

Things had changed a little; the tree was noticeably grander, although in general, things actually felt much smaller than my memory as a girl. I looked up at the sandaled, socked leg of my boy. It looked such a perfect, small, dark calf hanging down, his brown, well-worn Clarke's sandal unbearably cute. I caught sight of a tight, two-tone spherical bunch of mistletoe several branches beyond, sticking out as a very different growth to the sleek uniformity of an otherwise perfect oak. Ordinarily, the last thing one would think about on a summer's day, when up a magnificent tree such as this, was cancer. Certainly it was the first time I had ever thought about it up here.

The first alarm something was amiss was our neighbour's Cocker Spaniel jumping up on me as I sank into their rather doggy sofa, to enjoy a well-earned cup of tea. At first it was funny, he started nuzzling my shoulder and then my breast, but it quickly became a bit embarrassing and Sinead had to drag him, banned to the kitchen and close the door.

I thought nothing of it until two days later, slipping into a much-needed Radox bubble-bath, more tired than usual and afraid I might be coming down with something. But as I recalled the incident, my hand came to rest on my breast and I pressed the spot the dog had been digging at above my nipple. They tended to be a little lumpier whilst I was menstruating, but this lump didn't feel right.

It was Mum who persuaded me to go for a check however the doctor, like me, wasn't overly concerned, but sent me for a mammogram anyway, as a precaution. So began a life of waiting. Waiting and not knowing. My only experience of it previously had been waiting for exam results, but this had much more of a negative slant to it. Eventually, all one did was stagger from one set of results to the interminable interval for another, shredding month after month.

Seeking the sunlight through the oak leaves, I spied a spider sitting in midair, far enough away not to be a concern, square in the middle of an impressive web, motionless, save for the soft dip of the tree. The patience of a spider, to sit in wait through all weathers, to build, to rebuild, to wait and wait. Was there anything more focussed? More Zen, more committed, with more conviction than a spider? I knew waiting, but I had to concede, not like that. Could I allow a spider to be my role model?

I had waited for an appointment at the hospital, all the time suppressing the knowledge that it was important to catch these things early. The cold intrusion of the hospital visit sitting on the kitchen calendar like a slab, I made on my own. My breasts crushed cruelly by the machine, dealt with by a functionary rather than someone I would describe as a nurse. As if I was somehow unclean for even needing a mammogram.

More waiting and then another kind of scan, which also had the doctors frowning and an injection to help ease the pain, only serving to escalate my anxiety. On top of all this it somehow felt that I was at fault. That there was something I had done to bring this upon myself and that in doing so, I was a second rate citizen. But the overriding fear, my overriding concern I was pushing down with greater force but lessening success was Ash. Who would care for my boy, if not me?

It wasn't even a question over which to blub. It was just the most important thing on my mind. The obvious answer would always have been my parents and if things had been more straightforward, it wouldn't even have been a question, but adopting a coloured baby hadn't been their idea of a good plan. I knew for a fact that my mother, for all her good qualities, would never have countenanced going to see a Black doctor. And, if I was to be brutally honest with myself, if I had known how hard it was going to be, perhaps I would have thought twice about doing it. It was all very well thinking I was giving a baby a much needed home, but I hadn't even considered the day to day, the walking down the street and being stared at. Or even the need that the child had that I very early on realised I was unable to supply. I wasn't his mother and the look on his face, even at eight months old, made me understand that on some truly fundamental level, I never could be.

What followed will shame me for the rest of my life, although I realise now that his rejection of me fed into something very deep. It wasn't his fault of course, but his summary rejection led to a tit-for-tat rejection on my behalf and so a pattern emerged that seemed to all intents and purposes unbreakable. I saw now, with the magic of hindsight, that his rejection was perfectly normal; to be expected, but it slid its witches fingers straight into some terrible insecurity in me. As a child, my parents loved each other wholly, there was no greater love and it was still evident, even today; they were as one. But where was a young girl, the Gillian-come-lately, going to fit into that little equation? How would she ever avert her father's loving gaze to focus it on her, if only just for a moment? One plus one equals odd-one-out.

But it was difficult to blame perfect parents for such a glaring, black fault-line in me and sometimes the volcanic frustration I felt overwhelmed me. I had heard of people doing terrible things, blacking out and not remembering thereafter anything they had done, so complete was their apoplexy. I however, had none of that comfort, for I recalled with unerring clarity all of my transgressions, as well as the pain and surprise they elicited and yet I was completely unable to prevent it happening the next time, when I looked down at the need in his face for something I didn't have in me to give.

As Ash had grown older and the prospect of any real respect for me had receded over the horizon, I seemed set on fear as replacement, as if acting under a curse more powerful than anything I could do to counter it, the resultant shame creating a double-life; a smooth, ordered outer skin for presentment to the world, obscuring a complex reality underneath of molten emotions and a fat trigger all too easily tripped.

Like high beams on the darkest of nights, I found it all impossible to look at for long. But impossible to apologise? I sent apologetic waves up at his dangling legs. Wishing he could feel them, read my thoughts. Feel my own pain and anguish at having caused so much for him and his innocence. But even now, I couldn't be sure that there had been a last time. Even now, I couldn't promise him that. And so the waves of my apology faltered and shrank.

Each step in my treatment became more and more invasive; less easy to ignore, to pretend it wasn't happening. The next was a biopsy, taken with a handheld punch I wasn't prepared for, that hammered into me with a loud bang, drawing less blood than shock. As if finally punching me into the reality of my situation, perched on the edge of a high, paper-covered bed, an ill-fitting blue wrap tied poorly, four times up my back the only thing preserving what thin shreds of dignity I had entered the Oncology Ward with. I felt bludgeoned, empty and sick. It had to be ok, because I had a boy to look after, a boy that needed me. As my unsuckled breast turned an ugly hue with the bruising, I tried not to think of it as a portent of things to come, more a purging.

More waiting. Taking my mind off. Going through the motions of life as if all were normal, when it was anything but. Fencing previously inoffensive questions like 'How are you feeling?' 'Alright, love?' 'How are you today, dear?' with a small nod, a smile and an instant dipping of my eye line, designed to say 'I'm so fine, it's boring... nothing to talk about at all, thanks'.

Eventually, I had a call from the hospital asking me to go in. I knew something was wrong then, if they weren't going to talk to me over the phone. It was such a nice, sunny day as I minded the traffic, walked across the road, hopped the curb and slipped into the hospital. My meeting was with a surgeon with thinning grey hair glued to his scalp, who peered over his bifocals to say that the cells they had found were cancerous and that 'Grade Three' meant that it was growing fast.

Mum and Dad were away in the French Alps, so I didn't want to tell them and ruin their holiday. I had to try and put on a brave face for Ash, as children want to see how much they need to be upset. It's a tough call to make but, as you do it on and off throughout life for them, in the end, it's just another one of those times. Telling people bad news is grim; you feel responsible, invaded, definitely as if you are putting on an act. If you are lucky to have people around who love you it's both good and bad, because you have nowhere to go to just be sad. Scared. Shocked.

I hadn't expected it, but it was Dad who took it worst. I knew Mum would be stoic, but I had expected Dad to be strong too. It was harder seeing it through him almost than living through it myself. As if he somehow threw up a mirror by which I saw it all more clearly.

I had a lumpectomy to remove the tumorous part of my breast. After the operation I was tired, sore and had to have a drain put in. Before I felt I'd recovered properly from that, the chemo started. If I had been Grade One or Two I might just have got away with radiotherapy, or maybe not even that, just drugs. But with Grade Three, they decided I needed six lots, with three-week intervals. It was just after the fourth of these treatments that Ash got himself expelled from school.

It's so tough and different for everyone, but it gets worse as time goes on. The last one, they took pity on me, weakening dose as it hurt my head so much. It seems I have narrow veins in my arms and the drug damages them as it goes in – small veins means it takes longer for the drug chemotherapy to go in, done as it is through a needle, sometimes in your arm, your hand, or your chest, depending how they are behaving at the time. Injections would sometimes take three hours. As my white blood count became low I had to have additional injections once a day for a week to bring it back up. For someone with a morbid, lifelong dread of needles, I had thought this program was designed either to kill or cure me, but did neither and I remain resolute in my loathing of them.

My hair went very quickly. A couple of weeks after the start of chemo it came away in chunks over the sink. All of the pain I had endured up to that point I had done just that; endured. But the sight of my hair, locks coming away from my scalp as I mechanically passed my hand through it and thereby lift it off my face was too much and I am ashamed to say I wept into a fist of hair as I gripped on to the lip of the sink, but I swear, only for my boy. It was a terrible shock.

Directly after the chemo finished, I started radiotherapy. The Radiologist would take a while setting me just so on an unkind table in a cold room, instructing me not to move a muscle and then she would retreat with everyone else into another room whilst they blasted my boob as I posed, wondering how different this table was from the ones down in the hospital mortuary. Six sessions once a week, but by then, I felt so dehumanized, so weak, so beaten up by the excruciating pain of it all that none of it really mattered any more. They could have removed a leg and left me nakedly thumbing a wheelchair and it wouldn't have come as a shock or surprise.

I didn't feel like eating, I was exhausted, I couldn't sleep, my stomach hurt, God, even my bones hurt. Sometimes I itched all over, but beneath my skin, so it was impossible to scratch it away. I was restless, I looked yellow, hairless; I no longer recognised the hag in the mirror. Not even just physically. I mean even the eyes looking back at me, as if my soul had turned its back in disgust and gone and hidden somewhere to lie with itself, like some chastised dog.

They could have done anything; I would have endured anything so long as I knew that by the end of it, this thing would be gone, I would be cured and I would be well enough to make amends and see my boy through to adulthood; at least just 'til then. That was the deal I made with myself.

If I could have done it all in isolation it would have helped, because it was nearly always in the reactions of others, even individuals you didn't know, that you felt it most.

Now, some months after I had been given the all clear, battered but by no means beaten, they discovered it had spread to my liver and bone and the unending tangle, the Cirith Ungol of medical procedures, of appointments, side-effects and medication had enshrouded my life again, cutting out the light.

I felt dizzy and lay with my eyes shut, until it subsided. It had been a risk, coming down to Kent. I knew it would make me terribly weak and I was afraid of collapsing, or inadvertently crying out in front of him, but I'd so needed to see for myself, with my own eyes that he would thrive here, as I believed he could.

We stayed there a good while longer; the acorns stretched in their cups, the wax-plastic mistletoe sucked life from the thirsting tree and beyond, house martins dived a dogfight as I sat propped, listening to the music of an Ash in an Oak, happy in the knowledge that we, both of us right then, seemed content with each other. Mum banging the saucepan lid with her wooden spoon bringing us back down to earth and, linking arms we headed up for dinner.

Chapter XIII
  1976
  Impatient as I was, there was nevertheless a small
lull in engine production until Grandma was
guaranteed to be away for at least a couple of hours.
That opportunity finally arose when she went off for
a long-awaited appointment with the hairdresser,
combined with a visit to the church, to help organise
the impending harvest festivities.

  The moment she disappeared up the drive, Russ,
Grandad, Helen and myself swung into action. It was
trickier than I had envisaged, manhandling the MkXII
out of the stables, across the yard and into the
workshop. The trip from one to the other was easy
enough with the tractor, but getting it out of the
stables meant taking it off its rig, as it was just too
wide to pass out of the door. So getting it across the
stable floor, out of the door and, once across the yard,
reversing the process into the workshop at the other
end proved an education.

  Grandad had spent two days fashioning a trolley
with squat, sturdy wheels to make rolling it within
buildings easy. He also took the opportunity to put
another set of the same wheels on the engine rig
whilst it was free of its load. However, we were still
engaged in the last segment of the operation when
Grandma returned, but thankfully, the tractor was out
of harm's way and everything still remaining took
place behind the closed door of the workshop and I'd
never witnessed her cross that threshold. I'd begun to
realise quite how much needed to go into the simplest
of things. Rigs and organisation became the rule of
the day, every consequence needing to be considered
before anything was actually undertaken.

Once we had the two engines in the same room, it was easier to see what we had, what we required and therefore what was left to be done. Grandad's MkXII came apart a good deal easier than mine had, due to the fact that he had already taken it apart and meticulously cleaned, greased and oiled all the components, before putting it back together. This fact enabled me to familiarise myself with much of the mechanics, although I still had help and any of the larger pieces were always manipulated with two people present. It was exciting to be a part of the process, rather than merely an interested spectator.

It quickly became clear that although we were indeed able to mix and match parts from both to create a new, far more complete engine, there remained some glaring holes. The MkXII of course, didn't have a supercharger, it never had. However the one on mine was beyond mending, having been smashed with the brunt of the impact.

It was remarkable though, what condition the rest of my engine was in. Grandad seemed to think that it had gone into the ground 'quite gently', perhaps the combination of landing in water, then soft clay had saved it from much worse damage. The clay had done something else too, which was to provide an 'anaerobic cocoon' as he was fond of calling it. This had the effect of preserving the engine when, if it had been exposed to air, it might have corroded far worse.

This said, having been in the ground for 30 years, the oil inside the engine had actually also served to corrode elements of the Merlin from within as, over time, acid in the oil had attacked the metal.

Life on the farm also took over, including the cull. This entailed quite a few farm birds being slaughtered for the pot, however, I hadn't really comprehended what this truly meant until I awoke one morning not to the cockerel, but the cacophony of several alarmed farm birds in the stables courtyard.

Hurrying down to investigate, I found that many of the ducks, chickens and also some geese had been corralled in a vacant stable. In the courtyard just outside sat a squat, bark-free tree block, with the tip of a small but tasty axe stuck in it. There were also a few more unfamiliar faces milling around than usual, to help with the business. Grandma admonished me, getting me back in for some breakfast, but my curiosity was aroused. I needed to see what happened at a cull. As soon as I was able to, I jumped up and ran back around to the stables, however, what met me stopped me in my tracks.

I arrived just in time to witness two men I'd never seen before kneeling at the newly bloodied stump, one bringing the axe blade down on the stretched neck of a pinned chicken. The head bounced to the flagstones, a look of sickened disbelief on its face, its eyes half closing, as if trying to deny the catastrophe that had just befallen it, its yawning beak flexing, throating silent screams.

Once released, the body was in an even worse state. Thrashing wildly, it attempted to fly, to run away from the scene of the murder. Without its own head though, it managed solely to stumble, flap and crash into the wall, blind as it was, spilling gobbets of dark blood from its open neck. Yet still, it seemed so very full of life, full of flight for a couple of minutes, but its fight seemed so lamentably late. It was as if the life then ebbed from the body, as it sank fitfully to the floor, its wings flapping less and less coherently, claws making more and more spasmed, feeble attempts to deny the horror of its own demise, hiding its final shame in a heap in the corner.

But it was a gradual decline, as if, despite the head completely leaving the body and death presumably being instantaneous, the physical body hadn't actually twigged, or understood this key point of fact. As if it had arrived that morning expecting its day in court, to argue at a balanced hearing its case for life, but this option was taken from it far too soon and so it went through the motions anyway, like some macabre, wind-up toy. Soundless, but for the hapless flapping wings, an ever-decreasing dance of death as the coil spring unspooled; disjointed, the needle caught in a scratch. I'd never witnessed anything like it.

The poultry penned in the stable seemed completely aware of the horror about to befall them. I didn't need to see anything like it again and didn't stay to watch the next poor creature cornered, to have its neck stretched ignominiously across the altar. It had to be better than the shrew caught and toyed with by the cat, but even so. Life and death were very immediate on a farm and although Jet's stable door was ajar, he chose not to watch.

I felt a dreadful pang of shame at the recent memory of a hare I'd trapped. Armed with the rabbit snare Grandad had supplied me, I'd gone down the bottom field and duly set it up in what looked to me like a pathway cleared in the grass. For a couple of days I got nothing, so losing interest, neglected to check it. Then, one morning as I went down for the usual egg run, I espied a brown something in the grass. Going over to investigate, I found the long body of a hare lying on the track, very dead, rigor mortis set and looking alarmingly big. It had walked straight into the fine wire snare and presumably strangled itself in its vigorous struggles to get out.

I was repulsed by the carcass before me and even more so by my setting the snare to kill the blameless animal. I hadn't even wanted to catch a rabbit in the first place. It had only been a ruse to get out of a conversation I hadn't wanted to have. I'd known rabbits were a pest, so it had seemed like a good idea at the time, when I had been flailing around for something concrete to come back with, but I'd never considered I would end up snagging anything, let alone a hare. Standing there confronted by the reality of it, it seemed a truly grisly business altogether and I closed my eyes to it, physically shuddering at the fact that I had been directly, pointlessly responsible for this mystical creature's death.

There had been an excitement, a romance associated with the idea of laying a trap; the idea that one could outwit nature and actually capture something, without needing to think of the true consequences beyond that. Now that I stood over the body of this hare, it's sunken, unseeing eye half-closed, teeth bared in a garrotted grimace, all I could see was the absolute waste I had procured and wanted no more to do with it. I couldn't eat it and I didn't want a pelt. What was I doing?

I realised I couldn't just leave it there and have someone else come across it, so I slowly adjusted myself until I was able to gingerly extract it from the noose. Using a dock leaf as a shield, I then picked it up by the hind legs and tossed the heavy beast under the hawthorn hedge. The snare was a brilliant device.

So simple, just a smooth, woven wire noose with a couple of wooden pegs driven into the earth, it was super effective. But I never wanted anything more to do with one.

That afternoon, the playroom was transformed into some sort of abattoir larder, with ducks and geese arrayed upside down, hanging by their feet from the rafters. Two women, dressed in white overalls, hairnets and masks were engaged in plucking the birds in slow deliberate fashion and doors were opened and closed with great attention, to minimise the amount of feathers flying about the place. As I passed through on my way to the kitchen, one of the women reaching up grabbed a goose by the belly for purchase. The dead bird however, expelled a loud, unexpected honk, defiant to the last at its untimely demise, scaring the woman out of her wits and causing me, after the initial shock, to fall about laughing. This didn't go down too well, so I escaped to my tree with a Pilot's Handbook.

Chapter XIV
1976

Mum was in a bed in an older part of the hospital, where the ward seemed larger than usual. There was a subdued feel to it, where everyone moved through in a quiet, unhurried fashion.

She appeared to have lost a lot of everything; her face so pale, with bags under her eyes she'd lost weight and all of her hair. She seemed really pleased to see us as we appeared in the doorway, making our approach past several beds and the nurse, positioned at a table near in middle of the room, but her smile was only on her face, it didn't translate through her body, which remained resolutely attached to the bed. The nurse followed us over, propping her up with another pillow, once we had kissed our hellos. I was afraid to hug her. I didn't like the smell either and it was altogether too warm in there.

The patient in the bed directly opposite would moan periodically in a high-pitched, plaintive voice and then call for the nurse. But I could soon see that this was her default behaviour, that whatever could be done for her had already been done and she was just writhing in the jaws of an agony that wouldn't go away. A friend or relative sat, a little drawn back from her bedside, with the look of wishing she could disappear into the chair, embarrassed by the piteous cries of the prone woman. Covertly, I couldn't take my eyes off them both, even though I knew it was rude of me to stare.

Sensitive to the new guests, the nurse pulled the curtain around the lady's bed, closing off the view, but could do nothing to stem the wails. All this time, Grandad had been speaking quietly to Mum, holding her hand tightly against his chest. As she spoke, her eyes consistently drifted across to me, even though I could hear they weren't discussing me. It all felt awkward, distressing and I felt taut, like a trip wire and just wanted to get out. Get out and take Mum back home.

Turning to me, she asked ordinary questions, out of place with the circumstances, about how I was and what I did with myself during the day. Whether I'd made a start on 'Lord Of The Rings' yet. How the engine was coming along. Whether I was being a good boy. I was hardly likely to say no, was I? I never understood the point to that question; it just seemed so stupid. And yet, as she asked me, her eyes seemed to be beseeching me, having a whole different conversation, asking completely different questions of me, making me want to cry, but with tears of anger. Why did we have to be here? She was too young to die. It didn't make any sense and God was a bastard. I wanted to bite someone really hard, on the fleshy part of their arm.

We hadn't been there long and it was time to go. I couldn't bear to leave her but I couldn't stand to remain any longer either. It was awful and I cried blind into my elbow sleeve as Grandad held my other hand and steered me out of the hospital. I couldn't understand why all this was happening to me. To her. Maybe I was an Evil child. You didn't get given up by your mother if you were any good. Adoption wasn't special, it was only for the rejects, everyone knew that. And now my other mother was going too.

Gran visited her the next day and, as I pulled my shoes on to visit her the day after that, Grandad loomed large in the doorway. He didn't say anything because he didn't need to. She was gone. I looked down at the shoe I hadn't pulled on yet. There was no point in pulling it on now, but it felt so odd not to. I stood paralysed, wondering what to do next as my eyes filled up with tears. Grandad held me and I gripped the back of his shirt, pressing my face into his stomach, sure that if I pressed hard enough, it would all go away, she would come back, we would go home and she could beat me, pull my ear, my hair, kick my shins as hard as she wanted.

The funeral was a wretched affair. The spell of summer well and truly broken, the rain swept in unabated all day, as we rushed from car to church to clutch an Order of Service and sing hymns, punctuated by eulogies from the vicar and one of her school friends I knew as aunt Wendy. Front and centre, a coffin that bore no resemblance to Mum. No connection at all. I didn't believe for a moment she could be in there. It was then carried out to a hearse and we followed on to a crematorium, then rush back to the cars to adjourn to the hubbub of a pub backroom for food.

As I sat on an orange plastic chair among strangers, with one of Gran's sausage rolls crumbling at my lips, I never felt more alone. I made a vow I should never be lonely, if I could help it, for lonely was a horrible place to be. Everybody was nice to you, but their eyes betrayed them. I desperately wanted to see Helen, but she was on holiday. Russ was by the bar, but I didn't want him to see me.

I realised I hadn't cried all day. Not for the whole journey up there, not during the whole service. Everyone looked at me like I was going to, but I didn't. Grandad was in terrible shape. I think he avoided me because he felt so bad, or he thought it would be bad for me to see it and he tried to hide it, but there was no hiding that day. I expected Gran to cry, I suppose I expected Grandad to as well, but I hadn't pictured how he might cry. It was the most upsetting thing of the whole day.

Maybe I knew why she was dead.

Chapter XV
   1976

Gran and Grandad left early for Sunday Service. They had asked the first few times, but left me to my own devices since. I listened to the door close, the car doors slam, one and then the other, the car start and then make its slow progress up the drive. Breakfast was waiting when I went down and I sat munching cold toast and marmalade, looking at the woollen hat on my boiled duck egg, whilst Hamlet whined plaintively. He hated it when Grandma went off the farm without him and would often whine, looking first out of the window and then across at me, tall enough as I sat in a chair to look me straight in the eye, as if I would have some solution, or be able to talk 'Dog' and explain how long she would be, or better still, magic her back to him.

Outside, the wind harried the vacating trees and, having crept in almost unnoticed, autumn was now fairly at the controls, tearing outsized orange leaves out of the majestic, tiered chestnut trees to carpet the fat, cracked conkers littering the ground. Had I been at home, these would have been conkers prized above all, so full and dark were they. But here, now, there was no cause to covet them.

The air, even when still, had a cool expectancy to it and night was wasting no time in arriving, doing away with the long, extra hours that summer had seemed so generous with. Fruits, vegetables now harvested, hay bales again stacked all the way up to the eaves of the barn. The final rounds with the mower, the last of the gloss well dried and wind-hardened on various windowsills around the farmstead.

Getting up from the table, Hamlet skulked off to the lounge where he could better monitor the driveway, as I drifted through the kitchen to the playroom, switching on the jukebox. As I waited for it to warm up, I headed to the pantry and selected a raw raspberry jelly off the shelf, pulling the plastic open with my teeth, before sinking them into the fragrant red chunks, stretching and pulling a couple off with a good deal of effort. I sauntered back into the playroom, hit a few random song selections and then slumped backwards on the Den sofa to tackle the rest of the jelly, a fine cloud of sofa dust enveloping me, curling fingers into the still atmosphere.

Slowing down in the cooler air, houseflies had started congregating, using the lit bulbs as braziers, seeking out crevices in which to wedge themselves. Outside, great, rusty autumn spiders were busy negotiating massive webs across every conceivable gap not regularly broken by people or animals. I wondered how good their eyesight must be, that they could look across from a piece of farm machinery to a fence, an overhanging branch, fully ten feet apart, visualise their construction, make a super-thick thread, walk between the two without the silk snagging en route and then create their fine, intricate nets, capable of stopping a 7-inch leaf from hitting the ground. Perhaps the flies had come in purely to avoid the web mass-production taking place across the rest of the farm.

The Eagles- 'Best Of My Love' was leaking out of the speakers and seeping like a stain across the floor, when the door sprang open and Helen punctured the gloom by sticking her head around it. I sat up from my impromptu nest as, having checked the coast was to her liking, she took a step in, revealing a portable white television on the end of her trailing arm.

"I thought you could use this." She said.

I jumped up and studied it. I'd not seen a telly that small before.

"Is it yours?"

"Well, I was out scouting for bits and the man in the shop took pity on me and gave it up for two pounds. He said it only needed the cable replacing and a new plug."

I examined the plug-less cable and sure enough, there was a split three quarters of the way down, as if it had been crushed.

"That's fantastic. I'll get some cutters. I think there's cable and plugs in the stables."

"Or we can take the one off that one."

I wasn't aware she knew of the Den, or indeed, of the broken TV, come to think of it. I'd never given her a tour and, as she'd always seemed pretty reserved about invites, I'd given up asking.

"I'll get a screwdriver and some cutters. You can choose a song, if you want. It's free." I said, nodding at the jukebox as I raced out of the door. It seemed to take an Age to locate a suitable screwdriver, having found the cutters quite easily. I burst somewhat breathless back into the playroom, nervous that, like some butterfly, she might have changed her mind, but she was still there, bent over the turntable, knee swinging in slow rhythm to Freddy Fender's 'Before The Next Teardrop Falls', her face lit gold and red. I wish I'd put something cool on but, not expecting company, I'd determined several days before to mix in some of the singles I wasn't familiar with, this being one. I didn't like it.

"Two quid. That's pretty good for a telly." I said.

"Only if it works. He did say I could have my money back if it didn't." She made a selection on the jukebox, but I was unable to see what.

"I thought you might like to watch the Remembrance Day Service. Dad says they're having a fly past. Do you think, if we just use the shortened cable, put the plug on there... will it still reach the socket?" I realised I had completely forgotten the cable and plug.

She lifted the TV and, carefully clearing my forgotten jelly, plonked it in the dust atop the dead one, as I crawled behind with the end of the cable. There were all sorts of things back there. Two crushed ping pong balls as well as one good one (two star), a 'Great Expectations' paperback edition, bent permanently open at page 107, almost half a long, blue candle, a funny brooch, a miniature white porcelain cat with a black face and big eyes, a 1958 shilling and a yellow pencil with a worn rubber on the end. I shoved them all carefully out behind me as I made my way in and then, feeling a bit crushed, finally remembered why I was there in the first place.

"Yes. Just."

"Great." She cut the flex and I set about pulling the old TV plug out and salvaging it with the screwdriver. The driver was too small to work easily for the big screw, but perfect for the small ones inside, so I found myself improvising a bit. She always smelled nice. Clean, but in a kind of perfumed-clean way, not just soap clean. It was always so nice being close to her.

There was a pause in the soundtrack whilst the mechanism secured the old '45 to retrieve the new and then 'The Joker' bounced out of the jukebox, stepping jauntily over the corpses of my last two choices. Steve Miller Band, 1974. She was so hip. So dangerously hip.

I'd stayed up way past midnight. Who hadn't? But I didn't believe I'd ever 'toked'. I made a mental note; I needed to ask Russ what 'midnight toking' was.

"How are you getting on with the shopping list?" She said.

"Apart from the big stuff, we're still missing an Airscrew Constant Speed Unit, a Twin Delivery Coolant Pump and Intake, the whole Carburettor and Air Intakes, and the Twin Fuel Pump. Grandad's main concern is a lot of the seals. They all disintegrate over time and he says also the oil becomes really acidic and rots even metal, when it's left a long time."

"It's just so complicated, isn't it? So complicated. Try that."

She offered the cable, now with newly stripped copper, impossibly neatly twisted into perfect ears. I hesitated. I couldn't remember which one went where. She gently reached down, took hold of it and inserted the red wire under one of the screws, allowing me to tighten it up and complete the rest.

"My dad always said no son of his would ever leave his house 'without knowing first how to wire 'plug, drill 'ole, or change tyre ont car. Nor girl, neither'."

Her impression was both unexpected and so good we fell about laughing. I hadn't ever met her Dad, but

I could tell it was a brilliant impression. He was a northerner who'd made a huge amount of money from junk, travelled south and then married a penniless, posh socialite. Not many people liked him by all accounts and I confess not having met him, I was a little afraid of him, but he never bothered coming to visit Jet, sometimes dropping Helen off, but always at the end of the driveway.

The electrics complete, I crawled back behind the furniture and plugged it in.

As I took my time reversing out, I expected to hear her switch on, but she waited.

"Would you like to do the honours?" She said.

I repositioned the telly very slightly to face the sofa as she made herself comfortable, folding her legs sideways. I waited 'til she settled and pushed the button. A picture gradually sprang into life from the centre and she clapped. However, having filled the screen, the picture remained fuzzy and warped.

"Hang on." I twisted the aerial, trying to see the screen at the same time.

"There!" She said.

"There?" I let go really, really gently, so as not to disturb the force field and backed away. We had a TV.

"Oh. What channel? What time is it?"

"BBC…"

I twiddled the knob.

"Ah, it's started."

I plumped myself down on the sofa, only belatedly realising I was in very close proximity. I pulled away a little, but not much. There wasn't far I could go anyway without actually changing seats but she didn't mind, her attention on the monochrome picture of Whitehall; neat, raincoated rows of proud men, being joined regiment on regiment, some sporting double rows of medals, the monument already awash with a fluttering sea of dark poppies.

As the band played and the voice spoke of heroes remembering their fallen comrades, I welled up from nowhere and wept. I didn't even try to be quiet, I couldn't even do that. Helen reached out and put her arms around me, pulling me to her and I lay on her lap, wreathed in her embrace, bawling into the softness of her jumper. When I surfaced, she offered up a tissue and I withdrew self-consciously, desperately wiping the shame from my face in a vain effort to recover.

"It's ok. It's not easy to lose your mum."

"No. It's not easy." I said, so relieved that she understood.

I turned to the telly in time to see the camera tilt to the sky, as the sun broke through and the throb of six Merlin engines vibrated the box. The Lancaster Bomber, Hurricane and Spitfire of the Battle of Britain flight rolled low over the Memorial, their quivering, throaty hum throbbing into the distance, the commentator naming the three pilots.

"I thought we could go down to Baggett's Pond and lay some flowers."

"Ok." I said, pulling myself together with a bit of a quivery sigh.

We walked down in silence, gusts of wind blowing her hair about along with the leaves, but she didn't seem to mind at all. She took my hand, linking our fingers through and I made sure to walk in step with her. I wished Jet could see us now, but his stable door was bolted shut. The chickens and geese were unmoved, although I fancied Pinky and Perky were impressed, for they stopped in their muddied tracks and watched our passing. As we approached the bridleway, we separated to gather flowers from the hedgerow and then proceeded on down to the pond. The water had returned, along with some of the greenery.

She tossed the flowers, one by one into the water, as far as she could in the direction of the hole I had made in the ground, now invisible beneath the surface. It felt so long ago and a world away.

"I know he didn't go in there, but... well, it's all we have, isn't it?"

"Yes." I agreed.

"Shall we have a minute's silence?"

"Yes, let's."

We held hands again, bowing our heads slightly to look at the water. The wind blew through the trees as if restlessly impatient for big brother winter to come and finish the job autumn had started. The strewn flowers spread out, some partially sinking, others floating off in untidy Mikado clumps.

"You know, at my mother's service, I didn't cry."

I paused, glancing sideways nervously, but she didn't venture anything.

"I was so angry with her. For dying. But also..."

Helen waited a good while, but I had stopped utterly, staring at the small, white, sunken flowers in the water.

"Also what?"

"She used to hit me."

"I'm sorry. That's not very nice."

"No. I always thought it must be my fault. It was always my fault, doing things wrong, but then after a while I just gave up, you know, because I realised whatever I did, it wasn't ever right. She would just find a reason."

"That's awful."

The wind troubled miniature creases on the pond, depositing great handfuls of winged seeds whipped down from the supplicating branches. I wondered how many were wasted before one managed to land somewhere and make a tree.

"Don't tell anyone, will you?"

"No, I promise. Oh, you poor thing. So. It must have been good for you- coming here, I mean."

"I didn't want to. I didn't like it. I just.. I just wanted to look after her, you know?"

"That's pretty big of you..."

"She's my mum."

"Yes, I suppose, she's still your mum."

Suddenly it seemed pointless that the bright flowers were now dead and underwater.

"I found this tree I like to climb. I wanted to show you." I said.

"Where? I wondered where you'd sneak off to."

I led her back up onto the pathway and along to my Favourite Oak, the comprehensive carpet of leaves crunching under each footfall. The trees mostly denuded, you could now see the ancient oak quite clearly from the bridleway. She climbed very easily and I followed her up. As I went to go up another branch, she held my leg to stop me, so I sank down with my back to her, straddling the big, solid branch like a horseback made for two, gradually, eventually, leaning gingerly backwards until she simply scooped her arms under mine, pulling me bodily against her and into the tree. We nestled there against the wind, me resting my head on her shoulder, the smell of autumn swapping momentarily with her perfume and shampoo, hair soft against my ear, the largesse of her embrace enveloping me completely.

"Helen. I love you."

She didn't say anything, but she didn't move either; merely took a big, soundless sigh and we just sat, warm within each other, as the wind picked up everything it could manage and threw it about the place now the heavy hand of summer had at last relinquished its hold.

I toyed with writing a few poems over the following weeks, working very hard to find words that rhymed with Helen, but with little success, melon not really being the solitary result I was hoping for.

Helen gradually acquainted herself with more and more of the farmhouse. I felt like I was coaxing a wild deer in, gradually, slowly, with no sudden movements over a great deal of time; months, each encounter getting her to move slightly further into my domain. Now that I had her where I thought I had always wanted her to be, I realised I hadn't really thought through exactly what was meant to happen next. Currently, she lay on her stomach across my bed, chin on hands, looking around her as her feet swung in quizzical circles above the poetry of her knees.

"You've been reading a few books."

Rather than the doe, it was me who was feeling nervous.

"It's amazing. Things you'd never think. The Spitfire would be out of ammo in less than thirty seconds." I said.

"What do you mean?"

"When you pulled the trigger, they could only carry enough rounds to last for less than thirty seconds."

'I didn't know that." She thought for a moment. 'That's not very long, is it?'

"They used to carry cameras in the wing which would take a photo whenever the trigger was pulled, so they could verify a hit. But there was this one guy based at Duxford and he would come home and say he'd hit three bandits and they checked his footage and all they saw was empty blue sky, so they figured he was just lying. He would come back from missions and say he hit another one and everyone just thought he was, you know, just screwy and no one liked him, so they got rid of him by sending him to Malta. Then, when he got there, the whole island could watch the fighting up in the skies over the island and the sea and they loved this guy, cos he just shot down everything and became this big hero." I said.

"So why..? What happened? How did the cameras not see? Was it faulty? Did he have a faulty camera?"

"No. See, there's this thing called deflection."

"Deflection...ok."

"Yeah, see, when you try to shoot at a moving target, you can't just shoot at it, you know, unless you're really close, or directly looking at it, you know?"

"Ok."

"So deflection is when you sort of aim ahead of it, like where the plane is going to be in a few seconds, when the bullets get there, cos they take time to reach."

"Of course, you mean like clay pigeon shooting." She said.

"But they also fire tracers."

"I know tracers, they're ones that light up the path they're taking, right?"

"Yeah, so they made every fourth bullet a tracer, so you can see whether you're aim is any good and adjust, see?"

She nodded intently.

"So, with this guy, he was so good at working out the deflection, that he could shoot the planes out of the sky by aiming waaay ahead of them. He would study angles and speed and make all these calculations. I mean equations."

"So the camera…"

"So the camera would just take a picture of blue sky when he pulled the trigger, cos the enemy plane hadn't even got there yet. He could fire at them a long way away and they would run into his bullets like –over there. So he was this big hero for the Maltese, because they could actually watch him… see how good he was."

"That's amazing. That's a good story. What was his name?"

"Buzz. George 'Buzz' Buerling. He was Canadian. 31 kills."

"He shot down 31 German planes?"

"Well, not just German. I think a lot of them were I-ties too, over Malta."

"That's a lot."

"He got shot down four times himself."

"Buzz. I'd like to meet him. I like those names they have." She said.

"Me too. Can you imagine?"

We paused for a moment in our own thoughts.

"Ash 'The Bash' Wycherley. Ash 'Tach' Wycherley.. No... Ash 'Bosch Basher' Wycherley!" I said.

"Hels Bels Rutter." Unconvinced, we both pulled a face as our minds raced for better.

"Helen 'Melon' Rutter." She giggled helplessly at this one.

"Helen......"

"Helen...."

"Helen 'the Machine' Rutter. No... Helen 'Machine Gun' Rutter."

"That's quite good." I said. It wasn't quite right yet though and I was still no closer to finding her in verse.

A wood pigeon flew past the window in a big dipping curve and I shot at it with my Browning .303 machine gun.

"Ash. Has Russ said anything to you about me?"

"No. What sort of thing?"

"Nothing. Doesn't matter. It's exciting you going to Hendon, isn't it?"

"What do you mean? When?"

"Oh. Hasn't he told you? You mustn't say anything. Laura told me your Grandad was planning a trip up to London."

Chapter XVI
1976

That morning I was awoken very early, although as usual, the house was already a hive of activity. After a small breakfast I forced down, the better half of me still under my eiderdown upstairs, I was pressed to wash, dress, clean my teeth and be All Present and Correct in 5 minutes.

I wanted to go, it was just so early. Too energised to get off to sleep the night before, I was paying the price now. The idea of seeing a real, live Spitfire up close had proved too much. I had gone to bed early, lights out. Forbidden from late night reading, I had twisted and turned in my bed, watched the moonlight attempt to pierce the flowered curtains, casting its stark shadows from the window-frame, flowerpot and candleholder on the sill. Listened to Gran and Grandad eventually go to bed. They slept in separate rooms, but they didn't seem to mind about that. They were still getting on just fine. I had never heard them argue, or even raise a voice at each other, come to think of it. Eventually, unable to sleep, I had reached down for the torch I kept under the bed and shone it on the MkIX hanging from my ceiling, like a search-beam, hoping to catch an errant Gerry bomber.

Lying there, it was difficult to comprehend that I had my very own Merlin just yards away. I had to finish it. Mum wanted me to finish it. I had to show her I could do something and not mess it up. I looked up at the neat, elliptical wings above me. How would I make the rest of the plane though? Did Grandad have a complete fuselage secreted in the stables under a tarp that he would nonchalantly reveal the next time I cried into my greens? I suspected not.

I bundled into the car and, armed with a packed lunch of cheese and pickle sandwiches, tomatoes, an apple and a hard-boiled egg each, we headed for the station, Hamlet looking smug that he would have Gran to himself for the day.

The train rattled and shook its way up to London, through almost deserted towns and roads. Grandad was buried in a book and I contented myself looking out of the dirty window, undecided as to whether or not I was going to snatch forty winks. I noticed the inner sill was a graveyard of ladybird shells in various stages of crushed. As we slowed to a crawl in a cutting, there lay a fox curled in the undergrowth by the side of the rail, its bushy tail wrapped flawlessly around its entire body. It didn't even bother to lift its head, merely opening its eyes a slit, certain in the knowledge that the train was passing by, the same as every other one did and all the people aboard would just sit as I was, not doing anything about it, even if they noticed.

On arrival at London Bridge, Grandad gave me some change and sent me to get two underground tickets as he went to find a news vendor. The man peered down past his paper at me through the glass as I leant in.

"Two Hendon Returns, please." I said.

"New Delhi?" he asked, with an odd smile.

"No, HEN-don." I said. I hadn't thought you might be able to buy a ticket to India from here, I felt concerned that I wasn't going to be understood through the glass and end up paying a lot of money for a couple of useless tickets. How much might it be to get to India? Or was he joking? I turned around to see a sign of Grandad returning, but the man had passed tickets clearly printed 'Hendon' into the bowl beneath the glass. Being so long away from school, I'd forgotten how people could be. How I was often perceived. Being around Gran, Grandad and Helen had been nice, but it had also lulled me into lowering my defences.

We threaded our way through poster-lined tunnels to the Northern Line. I realised, after all this, I didn't actually want to go to the museum. I had liked the idea of it and all the time we had discussed it right up until this morning, it had seemed like a really exciting thing to do, but now, standing on the platform waiting for a train with a bunch of subdued people on their way to work, I really didn't see the point in it, unless Hendon were going to give me a working Supercharger and a Spitfire fuselage. I wondered whether Grandad had noticed the glances we'd been getting by people who must be wondering what our relationship was, this white old man with an Indian boy. To compensate for the guilt that followed momentarily afterwards, I figured it best to show Grandad some interest. I thought for a moment about a decent question that would set him off for a good while.

"Grandad, why would the 45's overheat in the air?"

"Ah, that's a good question." He said. I smiled back.

"The new supercharger was capable of 18lbs boost, which could overload the seals and lead to more leaking, you see… more leaking of coolant into the engine. Now, the pilot, he might see tell-tale white smoke coming out of the exhaust, meaning he was burning coolant, the temp gauge would begin to rise, quite quickly sometimes, depending of course on the severity of the leak..."

A train rumbled out of the tunnel and into the platform, precluding more information. I congratulated myself on my question; definitely a 9, if not a 10.

The carriage section we got onto had two people in it, a neat woman in a skirt suit at one end of the row and an extremely fat, completely neck-less man asleep on the same side, at the other end. We sat down opposite the man and Grandad, having had a moment to gather all the relevant details, had warmed up to his answer.

"The '45 supercharging was also prone to cracking the engine block." He continued. "Depending how big the leak was, by keeping an eye on the temp, really, that would dictate how long you had in the air before you needed to get it back on the deck. If you ran out of coolant, you probably had 30 seconds to a minute to get back down to the ground, but if you noticed early enough and pulled the engine right back, you could have a lot longer." Then, after a short pause, he went on down a twisty tendril about 'two-piece blocks solving the issue, but that they took time to disseminate through the RAF...' and I successfully tuned out as the doors slid shut, content that I might actually have stumbled upon the perfect question.

As the train moved off, Grandad in full flow, the man opposite stirred a little and I realised he was much the worse for wear, burping uncomfortably and dribbling a little. In fact, I had a sense he was probably still up from the night before. This was a new concept, something you really needed to be an adult to do, to be still up the next morning. Although that said, he didn't look like a good advert for doing so.

The carriage end-windows open, a wind-tunnel effect created an increasingly aggravated roar as we sped up, a crosswind rushing headlong through the train. Grandad pushed on, talking about compensatory improvements to much later Spitfire Marks and I leaned on the armrest toward him as though listening, however my attention was entirely absorbed by the specimen opposite. He was a big man, tall, but also incredibly large and, slumped as he was in the seat, his chest made a shelf under his stubbly chin which extended forward in a straight line to include his stomach, over which his pudgy arms were resting, almost at the same level as his chin. As the train lurched and swung through the tunnels, he looked increasingly queasy, even though he remained, as far as I could tell, asleep.

Then, he started to heave. His whole body getting involved in a ripple effect powering up from his gut, buried somewhere deep under the rolls of body fat, held in check only by the thinnest of stretched shirt material, like jelly poured into a plastic bag.

Just as I jerked sideways, in the immediate understanding that I needed to get out of the way, in direct line as I was, if he was indeed going to vomit - he did so. Still asleep, he really did so. His body convulsed, even without any conscious permission, his head rolling back slightly and then, gaping forward, jaw fully extended, a pressure hose of liquid sick jetted out of his mouth.

At that moment, there is absolutely no doubt that I would have been completely drenched in puke, frozen in mid-act as I was, if it weren't for one thing. The airstream, now fairly howling through the carriage picked up the deluge in mid-arc, even as I leant unmoving, staring at it coming toward me and threw it right angles down the carriage, spreading and scattering a little of it as it did so over the adjacent seats and floor, but the bulk of it was deposited, with surprising completeness, all over the pristine office lady sitting so neatly, ten feet away. She took a total broadside.

His discharge was almost entirely runny, with quite a few bits in it, rather than gooey, but an astonishingly copious amount and in the spewing served to bring the man around, his arms still crossed, resting on his belly ledge. He looked momentarily confused, perhaps disgruntled he'd been woken, then, licking his lips he realised he'd been sick. Looking for the result, his eyes travelled by degrees from the stretched shirt, bibbed in front of him, to focussing blearily on me but, although stunned into complete immobility by the theatre before me, I also remained entirely unblemished. He then turned his head slowly to his left, even as the last of his stomach's contents rose involuntarily out of his mouth, again whipping sideways and splattering the helpless unfortunate, several seats down.

For a couple of seconds, he looked apologetic, regretful, shamed at his stomach's behaviour, but registered simultaneously that there was simply nothing he could do about it, incapacitated and unequipped as he was. The lady meanwhile, had overcome her initial shell-shocked, rigid repugnance, her utter disgust, enough to retrieve a pitifully inadequate paper handkerchief from the now sodden handbag sitting on her lap and was wretchedly, angrily, desperately attempting to clean the most immediately offensive excesses of spillage from her face and neck.

It was as if someone had thrown a bucket of slurry down her from the right side. She was soaked, brown-stained all the way down one side, flecks of what looked like apple or tomato skin and brown stuff stuck to her hair, skirt, bag and jacket, all the way down the side of her right leg and yet the left side remained untouched. There was even a perfect outline of her profile on the glass panel to her left.

The channel of air pushing through the carriage was travelling at some velocity. Protected by the panes of glass at both ends of the seating, I had forgotten about it as fast as I had noticed it, once we had started to move off, but it had saved me. I looked down at my lap, my feet. But I was right, I was completely untouched by the onslaught when, by rights, I should have drowned in it. There might as well have been an invisible wall between us. If the train had been in a platform, I would have been buried but, as it was, this poor, immaculate woman sitting so beyond harm's way was now wearing almost all of it.

Judging by the point at which Grandad stopped talking, he woke late to what was unfolding before us. Likewise, he sat in stunned consternation as the man emptied the entire contents of his not insignificant stomach in two rounds and then returned to a semi-comatose state almost immediately after, a slightly more content look to his visage, happy no doubt to be rid of his queasiness. It all happened so fast. However, Grandad leapt into action and, diving into his bag, he produced a spare hanky, a packet of tissues and a rag in double-quick time. Avoiding the beer lake now swilling around on the wood-grooved floor, he passed all three over to the stricken lady, apologising as he did so.

Ordinarily, I imagine she would have refused his help, but so extreme was her situation that she received them gratefully and attempted some kind of clean up, at least getting the worst of it off her face, arm, hand and leg, before disembarking from the train. At this point, as the train slowed, the acrid stench of his misdemeanour reached my nostrils for the first time and I slammed my sleeve into my face to prevent retching myself. It made my eyes water. She nodded her thanks to Grandad and let out a stifled shriek as she ran off the carriage. I felt so sorry for her. We needed no further cue, unable to cope any longer, we too snatched at the opportunity to change carriages.

Through the entire episode, we didn't say anything to each other. It only took a tiny nod of Grandad's head for me to understand we were getting off and going next door. He didn't speak until we were pulling in to Hendon station.

"I think we can count ourselves very lucky back there, don't you?" he said.

"Yes. Very much." I exclaimed. 'I thought I was for it." Grandad chuckled. "Sometimes it's only luck that saves you." He said "And sometimes, it's aerodynamics."

It was the first time I had heard him laugh since Mum died, although it wasn't a full, belly laugh. But I felt relieved and closer to him for some reason for doing so. Laughs were hard to come by.

Hendon seemed to be stacked to the roof with aircraft of every description. It was almost overwhelming, but I just wanted to find the Spitfire. Grandad could sense this, but tarried at the Hurricane a moment.

"Can you see now, more clearly, the difference between a Hurricane and a Spitfire?"

I didn't need to be reminded of my mistake, a million miles ago, when I thought I had spotted a Spitfire flying over my tree; that Grandad knew nothing, but he wasn't trying to humiliate me.

"The Hurricane wing section is noticeably fatter, see? And therefore the aircraft is that much slower, but much more forgiving to the pilot." He continued.

"You see the exhaust stubs, they're shaped to give a little extra thrust at high speed."

"Right." I said.

"Even a few extra mph could make all the difference in a chase." He pointed to the bumpy fuselage.

"It has a Warren Truss construction inside... wooden formers, stretched over with doped Irish linen, the Hurricane is effectively a 1930's biplane without the top wing. Its design, its... heritage is a throwback to the old ways of making aircraft." He said all this, not with disdain, but there was nevertheless a lack of inspiration as he described it. He walked on and as he did so, he lit up. We had moved over to the Spitfire, a Mark IX, judging by the four-pronged propeller.

"The Spitfire on the other hand, with its *aluminium* frame, is a 1950's jet aeroplane, without the jet. *That's* the difference in the technology. So even though they have the same engine, the same instrumentation even, that is all they have in common."

I nodded seriously. It was a terrible mistake to have made, I realised that now. They really were completely different planes. He moved on, indicating the smooth metal fuselage.

"Spitfires were a completely innovative design. Aluminium-clad metal ribs. No two ribs the same. During the war, there was a drive to get everyone to hand in their old pots and pans for the war effort, so they could be melted down to make Spitfires. It was futile of course, as the ally wasn't good enough quality to be used in aircraft construction. Now, see here, looking down the fuselage, what do you notice? Look closely." I did so, but was clueless as to what he was wanting me to see.

"Look at the rivets." I looked closely.

"Some of them are flat and some of them stand proud, you see?"

"Yes." I said, immediately seeing. Some were indeed flush to the side of the aircraft and others were bulbous, standing proud.

"When they were designing the aircraft, they were trying to make it as streamlined as possible, obviously, but the flat rivets were problematic because there was less metal holding the skin on, so there was a distinct danger they would fail. The round ones were much more preferable. So what they did in tests was to glue individual split peas over the flat rivets to see which ones interfered with the airflow and which ones didn't."

"Split peas?"

"That's right." He looked very pleased. It was amazing. Who would have thought to come up with that? Maybe Gran. I wouldn't.

I stared at the aeroplane. The majesty of it. The clean, beautiful curved lines.

"It's said that the only straight line to be seen on the outside is the rails for the canopy." He said, reading my mind.

"It's also been said that the Spitfire is the 'second most pleasing collection of curves known to man'." I smiled, looking up at him quizzically, knowing that I should be getting something.

"Helen..?" he said.

"Oh." I grinned. Yes. Of course.

I pointed to the tray on the floor beneath the nose. There was a pool of dirty liquid in it; a definite leak.

"If there's no oil on the outside, there's probably no oil on the inside." He said in response. I moved over to the information.

The advantage between the Spitfire MkI and II over the Messerschmitt Bf109E was perilously slim, as had been demonstrated through repeated skirmishes in the Battle of Britain, during the summer of 1940. To this end, the MkIII was designed, incorporating a Merlin MkXX engine. However, it would take considerable time to manufacture and roll the new Spitfire out and there were also problems with the new engine, so the Air Staff asked Rolls Royce to come up with a stopgap. Their solution was to install the Merlin 45 into the Spitfire MkI airframe, so creating the MkV.

From 1941-43, over 6,500 MkV's were built, the Spitfire MkIII never rolling into production, its design later being superceded. However, some of the

*improvements   intended   for   the   MkIII   were
incorporated into the MkV.*

"Shall we go over to the library? We might be
able to find out something more about your plane."

"Right."

We headed out of the hangar. I already felt much
happier that we had made the effort in coming here, if
only to see Grandad happier. I hadn't wanted to seem
less than enthused in front of him, seeing how
dreadfully he had taken Mum's passing. It was nice
to feel he was doing something that took his mind off
it all, if only for a while. Mum would have liked that.
And she would have liked me doing that too.

As we walked between the buildings, he snuck a
hand over my shoulder.

"You know, your Grandmother and I are very
pleased to have you stay and I'm not just saying that,
we really are. And if we can't find a school that will
take you, I don't care. D'you understand?"

I nodded. A lump appearing in my throat, but he
didn't stop or break stride, just held the door open for
me and we walked into the library building.

It became evident that we had an appointment and
were expected. The man behind the desk looked over
his half-moon specs at me with a special smile. He
led us to a table where three books were already laid
out and explained that these were the Combat Report,
diary and logbook we were looking for.

Grandad sat me down, speaking quietly as he did
so.

"You have a look at these, I'm going to look into
the exact circumstances. You find anything
interesting, remember it, or write it down and tell me
when I get back. I'll be just over there."

I pulled off my coat examined the covers of the books arrayed. They didn't look all that promising, thin, old and covered in fingerprints as they were. Maybe I got the short straw as usual. I wondered what might be so interesting that it had taken Grandad across the room.

On the top sheet it said: -

Flight Sergeant Rudranath 'Rudy' Maharaj
Kills: five and a half
Me110 bomber
Me109
Half Heinkel 111
Heinkel 111
Ju88
Me109

Chapter Seventeen
1976

'Flight Sergeant Rudranath 'Rudy' Maharaj'. So, there it was, that was his name. And he was an ordinary man, not an officer. An ordinary *Indian* man. I knew very well that India contributed to the war, a great many men, but for some reason hadn't ever thought of them flying Spitfires from over here.

The Personal Combat Report was very factual, giving the dates, the squadron, the aircraft number and then the barest of facts about the missions- height flown, duration- and then a little more skeletal information if there had then been any enemy contact. There was a narrative at the bottom, which went into more detail of the sortie, but again I found it all a bit uninteresting, facts and figures, rates of climb, even though I knew it shouldn't. I glanced up, in case my disinterest was being observed, but the librarian was absent from his post. I could come back to it. I again wondered what Grandad was doing. I could just make him out behind a wall of shelves.

Along with the Reports were some photocopied pages of a handwritten book, remounted within a stiff card cover. Inside, there was a small black and white picture of a pilot posing beside a Spitfire, one leg up on something just out of shot. It all looked rather relaxed, not a combat shot at all, he had a woolly jumper on and an RAF jacket over the top, a shock of wavy, black hair but no cap and a cigarette locked in his lips.

His forehead was creased, a tight, lopsided smile on his face, but looking slightly to right of camera, as if someone else had spoken, taking his attention whilst he waited for the photographer to snap the shot. Rudranath Maharaj, so this is what you looked like. With a little difficulty, I mouthed his name to myself, so I should better remember it, glancing up momentarily; nervous that anyone might think I moved my lips whilst reading. The Spitfire in the picture was too close to read any details on the side, but it definitely was a Spitfire and there was the smallest bit of nondescript airfield behind and a cloudy, troubled sky above. But there was somehow a great kinship between the man and aircraft, even though he wasn't actually hugging it or anything.

One of my earliest memories was being given a green balsawood aeroplane for my fifth birthday. I loved it so much. It fascinated me, a big step up from the simple gliders I had had before, because this was a real plane, with a cockpit and a hollow fuselage containing an elastic band stretched from the tail to the white, plastic prop. By carefully rotating the prop in the right direction with one finger, you wound the elastic band until, knotted along its entirety, the prop cut into your finger.

Turning to face the wind, you could then launch it with a gentle throwing action, releasing the propeller as you pitched it and it would take flight, the elastic powered prop pulling it forward, slight adjustments to the tail creating just the right amount of lift. It even had small wheels on wires. But, as with all the gliders that had gone before, it eventually succumbed to the unreachable upper branches of a tall tree, a victim of its own success. Come to think of it, it could only have been Grandad to have given me such a present. That made me smile. It was like hearing a joke where you got the punch line (seven) years later.

The copied pages appeared to be diary entries and, with a little more scrutiny, I realised with a small shock of excitement, that they were the pages pertinent to all of the kills that Flight Sergeant Rudranath Maharaj had recorded.

After 12 uneventful sorties over Kent, London the South and East coasts, my first three tallies materialised the same day.

Scrambling to meet a wave of bombers coming in over Margate, we managed to get the jump on them and swung down from 15 Angels to engage with a flight of 20 bombers in strict, tight formation. Another flight of Hurricanes had the same idea as us and the bombers scattered under our combined attack, four being hit, although none by me. I managed to overshoot quite badly due to my own poor discipline, approaching over-excited and far too fast.

Pulling out of the descent, I came upon an Me110 bomber that had also dropped low out of the fracas and, approaching it with some latent speed above from the port side and with an eye for any covering 109's, got in close enough to give it a short burst. Better this time, I caught the starboard engine, which immediately caught fire and he dived away. Keeping an eye on my tail and above for possible bandit fighters, I followed, hoping to get a second burst in, when the Me110's wing snapped at the burning engine, so steep was his dive. I saw just one man bail out before the aircraft hit the ground.

Gaining height and with a little more confidence, I went back in, pleased that I still had enough ammo to have another go. As I climbed, coming straight towards me was a Hurricane in a dive, being hotly pursued by a 109. Missing each other by less than 20feet, the resultant slipstream hit me with quite a jolt, but I engaged with the following Me as it dived down at me, giving him quite a surprise. I saw my tracer hit him head on, straight through the prop into the engine and the glass of his cockpit, passing just under my nose as I pulled up to avoid him, our combined speed something in excess of 750mph.

Bursting into flames, he Roman candled and I saw no parachute, before the aircraft hit the deck. Poor bugger. I took a look around, wanting to re-engage, still with some ammo left over and plenty of fuel.

I spotted an Me and banked hard to drop onto it, but it saw me early, taking evasive action. Pulling round and fast out of my dive, conscious not to travel for long in any predictable fashion, I caught the tail of a dogfight. A Hurricane had seemingly emptied its Browning's into a Heinkel, which was leaking a fine line of glycol from one engine, but looked to be travelling fairly unfettered by its injuries. As far as I could tell, the Hurricane appeared out of ammo, so I tailed them both, one eye ever on my rear view and above, as I pulled the Heinkel into my sights. Even as I did so, the glycol fire in the starboard engine began to increase, the aircraft listing slightly. I paused a bit longer, just to get the portside engine clear in my crosshairs and then opened up with the last of my own ammo. Black smoke billowed obligingly under my ministrations and the plane didn't recover from its dive. The canopy sprung and I saw two parachutes before the aircraft hit.

Although I saw a fair few enemy aircraft after that, my next kill didn't happen for another 16 sorties, during which time I also spent much of my time training young pilots. Often, just our presence in the air was enough of a deterrent, bombers jettisoning their loads and splitting up, allowing them enhanced mobility to scuttle back across the channel to safety. But it was frustrating not to add to my tally.

Returning from bomber escort duty over France, with the sun sinking to my port side, I saw something glint down to my starboard side. Flying low-level, back towards France were a couple of Heinkel 111s. They were very low, around 1000ft and must have been on a hit and run mission somewhere along the South coast. I'd used up perhaps half my ammo, fruitlessly chasing Me109s over France, so was feeling pretty peeved not to have taken one down earlier and, checking I had what looked like just better than borderline fuel, if it was a quick hit, I figured it was worth a go... a possibility to make amends. We were closing on each other pretty fast, so I needed to make some quick decisions. I guessed they had to see me quite soon, if indeed, they hadn't already. I reckoned that, if they thought I had seen them, they would split, dropping even lower, camouflaged as they were against the darkening shadows of the water, whilst still nevertheless vectoring for the safety of the French coast.

As I peeled off my mask, my guess proved correct, for just moments after I had worked out their best move, they split as if on cue, diving away both left and right, but I had already determined to intercept the one that dived to his port side. Corkscrewing my

Shrew hard over in a rolling loop and throttling back, I was right onto the back of my Heinkel, now skimming barely a couple of hundred feet above the water, a sitting duck at that speed and with no agility at all to speak of, he had already played his best card.

Ignoring the machine gun bursts off the mid-turret, I closed fast, waited for him to fill my sights and then let him have a full, ten second burst that raked across the port engine, wing and into the fuselage just behind the peculiar glasshouse canopy, the smell of cordite filling my cockpit. On fire even before I had completed my strafe, he went down incredibly fast and, with no room for manoeuvre, broke up as he hit the water.

I couldn't see the other one anywhere, couldn't have had any ammo left to speak of and was now low enough on fuel to feel anxious, so hightailed it back to home, pleased to have added to my tally. I later found out I had sustained 23 hits myself to the fuselage and port wing. I got lucky. I honestly hadn't noticed it at the time, so intent I must have been on hitting my own target. It was hard blocking everything else out enough to focus on the kill. I found it to be the moments I was most likely to get jumped myself.

I paused in my reading. I had always assumed that fighters must have ordinarily shot down dozens of enemy planes. With so many pictures of Lancasters-whole walls of bombs denoting a hundred or more sorties, proud bomber pilots standing with rows and rows of bombs depicted under their canopy. I hadn't considered five kills as a big tally before now. But, beginning to understand the problems of flying, of aiming, of not having unlimited firepower, of being shot at even whilst shooting at someone else, it made five confirmed kills seem a lot. The advantage was indeed not so great between aircraft on either side, whatever the propaganda.

The Junkers-88 I met quite unexpectedly on a routine scouting party with Venting as my No.2, up the East Coast. Opaque sheets of winter rain were closing in across the North Sea and we had dropped substantially down in height in an effort to maintain visibility. I spoke to Control, agreeing that we would curtail operations and return home earlier than planned, due to the inclement weather. Accordingly, we circled round just north of The Wash. But as we drew a slow, wide arc, having turned to starboard out over the sea rather than inward overland, just as I was reflecting on the iron grey, forbidding view, the sky meeting the sea with no visible join, Venting spotted two Junkers 88 flying slightly above us and heading up toward the North coast; most likely reconnaissance aircraft.

I took the unusual tactic of attacking up from underneath and slightly to the side, as this was the natural and most economical angle of engagement when taking into account our current attitude to each other. With the Spitfire being so much faster, it made sense to bounce them as quickly as possible, before they had any chance to react, thus making some kind of impact, then kill off the lame aircraft once they had at least sustained an opening salvo. The weather really precluded any more elaborate plan. Cautioning my Number Two to be alert for any accompanying Messerschmitts and to wait until he had his sights full before opening up, I gave him the nearer of the two. They were certainly surprised by us. Venting hitting his Junkers fractionally before I turned off the safety and pressed the trigger on my own, watching as Venting successfully took out the port side engine, all thick, black smoke and flames, as it veered away in slow motion shock.

Waiting until I was only 200yards from the ugly, slow-moving target before squeezing the button, I hit mine using cannon only, the heavy recoil punching back into the airframe, a powerful, satisfying jarring in my seat, man and machine. As I closed, I could see the cannon rounds pounding black holes into the fuselage, directly where I pictured the crew should be. Without even a wisp of smoke, the aircraft tipped right over in a slow arc above me, plummeting with all hands upside-down into the waves, at almost the precise moment that Venting's splashed, less than five hundred feet apart. It was his first kill. He'd claimed half a Ju-87 before, but this was his first outright and he was delighted.

Mission successful. Two confirmed knocks, we turned tight, grateful to be back over terra firma and on our way home.

Even as copies, it was slightly weird to think that all those years ago, the very pilot that had flown my engine had created these pages, written in his hand. Had laid them blank on a desk and filled them with this neat, old style handwriting, with ink from a pot, very few bits crossed out or corrected. Small ink spots and blots, even what might have been a tea stain from a cup- all telling yet another story, overlaying the one written in ink, making the words human, as if he had written them yesterday and just stepped outside the library door to take some air and squint at the weather.

One of the most pleasing things was when you managed to catch enemy fighters. Surprising bombers was one thing, but getting the lead on an Me was always choice.

A good part of patrolling was to be there as a deterrent, but every now and again you would come across the very thing you hoped for and dreaded. But this time, we were cruising around 28,000 feet. In ideal position, with the sun behind us we spotted the enemy bombers first and then, above and behind them, the expected Messerschmitt escort. We had them outnumbered, Red Leader electing to go in first with Blue, leaving me with the bombers beneath. Tally-ho and we dived. Sure enough, the Me's engage, duly split into disparate dogfights and we descended through to the bombers beneath, already alerted and beginning to scatter, themselves.

I was by now in the habit of viewing the rear view as much as what was ahead and sure enough, I'd picked up a tail. Alerting my No2, I aborted my target and immediately threw myself into evasive manoeuvres, before he was close enough to get off any meaningful burst. Sweeping back up and nervously rubbernecking over both shoulders for my no2, as much as my pursuer, I could see the sky full of trails above me, each telling their own story. There were already four parachutes swinging in the air. They were all right, they were out of it.

Swinging back up, I spotted the tell-tale yellow nose of a bandit above and slightly to my starboard side. As sure as I could be that I had shaken my amour, I pulled around, lining him up. I was pretty sure he hadn't spotted me, as he made no move to change speed or vector. This one was mine, I checked wildly about me, but although the air as filled with planes of various shapes and sizes in all directions, I could see nothing on me. He saw me, but saw me late. I had waited and waited as per usual, for his form to completely fill my sights before opening up on him.

His late manoeuvre wasn't enough to save him, only change the point of contact that my machine guns made with his fuselage, cutting the tail off his aircraft as he pulled up hard in his desperate effort to get out of the way. No longer airworthy, he turned tip over tail in slow motion, dropping out of the sky, his canopy flying off as he negotiated the awkward clamber out.

Although I went looking for it, I saw no more action after that encounter, but was pleased with an out and out clean fighter scalp.

Belatedly understanding that I would find out about his final flight and therefore the circumstances surrounding my Merlin ending up in Baggett's Pond, I switched back to the logbook, flipping impatiently to the last entry.

'*Test flying the new MkV Spitfire, with a Merlin45 engine, Rudy was witnessed by his fellow pilot in a long, steep dive that he eventually attempted to pull out of, but at that point the aircraft spontaneously disintegrated in the air.*'

That would certainly explain why there were no other parts of the aircraft attached to the power plant, but why? I read on.

'Flight Sergeant Rudranath Maharaj failed to employ his parachute and died from the injuries sustained by his fall of approximately 800feet.'

How terrible, just dropping out of the sky like that. Perhaps he knew nothing about it. That would be best. I wondered what I was going to tell Helen.

I looked up as Grandad approached and showed him the photo, but only reported my findings once outside, over cheese and pickle sandwiches. He brought with him his own intelligence, explaining that the centre of gravity of a Spitfire -the balance of the aircraft- was critical and, in the case of Flight Sergeant Rudranath Maharaj, this was to prove crucial.

With the evolution of the aircraft, many were having more and more equipment stored in the fuselage cavity directly behind the pilot, greatly affecting the balance and therefore the handling of the plane. On top of this, some of the early aircraft employed hollow bolts to attach the wings to the fuselage, in an effort to save weight.

But, with these more powerful supercharged engines and resultant increased forces, when the pilot pulled back hard on the stick at maximum Gee, the aircraft could, literally, come apart in the air, structurally unable as it was to cope with the change in weight distribution, the increase in power, or the weaker bolts holding the wings on.

Wings had also been known to snap at the cannon point. During the war, aircraft developments were happening very much on the hoof, without the luxury of time to test things sufficiently and different departments not conferring on topics as much as they would have in peacetime.

So that was what had happened. The plane had simply been pulled out of a terminal dive only to come apart in mid-air. How awful. I started on my hardboiled egg, cracking it on my knee as Grandad had, peeling it carefully.

"Grandad, can you tell me, why it was called a Shrew?"

"I'm sorry?"

"Well, when I was reading Rudy Maharaj's diary entry, he called the plane his 'Shrew'." I bit the top of my egg and sprinkled some salt on the yolk.

"Ah, Shrew, yes. Well, that's interesting, because, originally the aircraft was destined to be called a Shrew, not a Spitfire at all."

"Really? A Shrew?"

"Then the boss of Vickers, I think it was, he decided to name it after a woman he knew, who he described as a real spitfire… and the name stuck."

"That's how it got its name?"

"I believe so. A good thing, no?"

"Yes. Supermarine Spitfire sounds a lot better. Supermarine Shrew…"

"Funny that Maharaj called her a Shrew though." He said, looking down at me. "Are you pleased we came?"

"Oh, yes. Very." I said. And I meant it.

"I wasn't sure…" he said.

"No, really. I just don't understand why he was in a steep dive for so long. He wasn't in a dogfight or anything."

"Well, we'll perhaps never know the answer to that. But a fair few pilots died due to basic errors. A great many. However, he was a very experienced pilot and even taught young officers how to fly, so that would seem unlikely. I don't know." He bit carefully into his tomato, not wanting to squirt pips.

"And I don't know what I'm going to tell Helen."

"Yes, of course. Well, I would always recommend the truth. I'm sure she will ask."

"Yes." I didn't know why it was so important to me that the pilot had survived this particular episode and lived to fight another day. It was as if it was all tainted if he died. Not enough to deter me, I was just concerned that it might turn Helen off the whole endeavour and I didn't want that to happen under any circumstances.

Lunch finished, we sat in the sun for a while, neither feeling the need to go anywhere or do anything other than let lunch settle. Grandad was a great one for letting meals settle.

"I didn't know Indians flew Spitfires."

"That was a surprise. Ash, you know he was Trinidadian."

"The same as me!"

"The same as you. You know, there were 7,000 volunteers from the Caribbean who served in the RAF, over 400 of them aircrew and over 180 from Trinidad alone, the most of any Caribbean island. There was even a squadron called the Trinidadian Squadron- Squadron 74, due to a contribution of Spits from the then Governor of Trinidad -and 139 I think, was Jamaica Squadron."

I looked sideways at him. "How do you know all this?"

"I only looked it up just now, when I found out his name." he grinned.

"I'd no idea there were quite so many Caribbean pilots- and so many medals. I knew they'd contributed, but I was more familiar with the Canadians, Kiwi's, Aussies, Czechs, Poles and the like." He added.

Then he put his hand on my shoulder and said, "Volunteering, coming from all the way over there, leaving their families -all they knew- behind... they weren't just The Few. They were The Very Few."

"The Very Few."

The trip home was far less eventful than our trip there, but I didn't notice it at all, preoccupied as I was with my own thoughts about Rudy, my Merlin and the revelations about my aircraft's doomed last flight. It wasn't until we were in the car, on the last leg from station to farm, that I ventured another question.

"Will we be able to build the rest of the aircraft?"

Grandad looked over from the driving seat briefly before answering.

"I was wondering when we would get around to that." He paused, smoothly dropping a gear, taking a corner and accelerating before continuing.

"I'm an engine basher, not an airframe rigger. I don't have those skills... that knowledge. And it is a specialised knowledge."

"No. Yes." I said.

"And, even if I did, do you realise how long it would take to build a Spitfire from scratch?" He looked over again. "It would take one man 30 years to build a Spitfire. That's how many man-hours it takes. So, even with three people -who knew what they were doing, which we don't- but even with three people, it would take ten years. That's a long time, Ash. I'm sorry. But that's the long and the tall of it."

I sat contemplating this.

"Let's just try and get the engine working, shall we?"

"Yes, let's." I said.

Chapter 18
1976
Following Gillian's death, Ash's overriding focus indeed became the completion of the Merlin. I didn't want to stand in his way, relieved that he had something to occupy him so fully. It may have been his circumstance, it may have been the discovery of the pilot's identity. And even though he was no blood of mine, he remained the last really tangible link to my girl and I realised for that reason alone, I would do absolutely anything for him. Only he had stopped Laura and I from collapsing; drawing up the drawbridge and closing in on ourselves.

His new friend Helen Rutter helped a great deal as well, accompanying him on missions to junkyards across the county, even as far as Sussex, in a concerted attempt to obtain the final bits of the jigsaw. I had already started giving him pocket money, but upped his allowance, and gave him ten pounds for his birthday, secure in the knowledge that he would only be spending the money on aircraft parts, or the journey to and from.

He proved a canny negotiator, obtaining pieces for a fraction of the price I would have paid, should I have been the barterer. I didn't know whether it was just her, or because as a team he and Helen complemented perfectly, or if it was the undeniable, earnest sincerity that often shone out of his face, so far from the boy I'd known, but whatever it was, it worked.

By December, word had got out there was a young Indian boy down in Kent on the hunt for aircraft spares. The local press got wind and, after a phone call, sent down a reporter to cover the story, which then went national a couple of weeks later. All kinds of things came out of that, with people offering pieces of Sopwith Camel, a complete Halifax bomber and even a working Gloster Javelin jet engine, much of it free if we were guaranteeing to get them working and not merely gathering for scrap.

I could see no harm in it. If it meant that Ash got his story out there and it turned up the missing components, so long as the reporters were sensitive to what had just happened, it could only be good for him. It also took the pressure off me a little, allowing some down time, some space to reappraise the situation we found ourselves in. I knew very well he wouldn't rest until it was complete, but I had a strong notion that it wouldn't end there and I needed a plan in place for when the inevitable happened and we completed the Merlin. How that eventually worked out though, was in a most unexpected fashion.

Sometime after the story had broken nationally, with Ash and his Spitfire the talk of the village for a couple of weeks, things had then died down, with no real strides made, besides my unexpected introduction to a small, countrywide network of retired Merlin Engine Fitters.

Through this, we did pick up several spares for components we actually already had, but also some valuable seals. However, the main piece we lacked remained the supercharger. Two had come to light as a result of the press, one all the way up in Lincoln but, after the initial excitement, a phone call proved one of them to be incompatible and the other no more than a useless, rusted lump, in no better shape than Ash's original. Even so, I needed to persuade him not to waste any money buying them anyway, but to wait for the real thing to turn up.

Christmas gave him a temporary diversion. We splashed out and got him a Chopper bike. Using clothes pegs, he wasted no time attaching cards to the rear forks and rode it around the yard, unsettling the geese, until I suggested he could now make it down to the shop. He returned with a comprehensive goodie bag of assorted sweets, but didn't neglect to offer them around.

Then, one day in early January, the phone rang, a gratifyingly loud Northern voice announcing itself over the other end. It was Helen's father. He had very little to do with the farm, his wife Annabelle always paid Jet's stable rental and upkeep well in advance and I knew he was well to do, but had only met him once in passing. I had been scrabbling for a hearing aid, but realised I might manage without.

"What's this I hear about your boy there and a Spitfire, Ted. Is this true?" His opening gambit.

"Oh, ah... Ash? Well, yes, he's attempting to rebuild one- we both are. But we're still missing some components..." I said, not really expecting much more of it. I didn't know where Helen was, if that was who he was after.

"Is everything alright?" I enquired.

"Why shouldn't it be?" Came back the response.

"I thought you might be after Helen... she's not here. At least, I don't think she is…"

"No, no, no. What I'm cross about is the fact that she didn't come to me about this. I get back from Miami and the first I learn of it is her face in the local rag and my neighbour telling me all about it. Now Ted, my father- her Grandfather, was a pilot in the

War and she bloody well knows this, so why she hasn't come to me and asked for help, I shouldn't like to guess."

This set me back. I had no idea about any of this and, if what he said was true, it was indeed a mystery, as she had proved so helpful in every other way, even spending her own money on a couple of bits herself, quite apart from the hours she had spent poring over the engine with Ash. But then, who knew the relationships people had with their parents, with their offspring. It was best not to get too involved in that particular minefield, of that I was certain.

"Well, I'm not really very sure. I wasn't aware of any of this. She's certainly been very helpful though. She's a very polite, well-brought up girl, I must say. A credit to you, if I may say." I added. This had the desired effect of taking the wind out of his sails a bit. There was certainly no reason why any right-thinking man wouldn't be proud to have her as a daughter, of that I was also sure.

"Aye, well, that's as maybe." He said. "I'm just a little upset that she would keep this from me, you know. It's unexpected and, if I may say between men, a little hurtful, I'll be honest with you, Ted."

"I see. Well, I'm sure the oversight wasn't intended that way. I'm sure you're a very busy man, Mr Rutter."

"Yes, well. Look… as you may well be aware, I'm in the business of junk. Junk is my business and I have done very well by it. There's not much about junk that I don't know, do you understand?"

"Yes, Mr Rutter."

"Not only that, I have an interest in certain aircraft parts and one of them 'appens to be the Spitfire. Now then. Am I given to understand that you are in the market for some Spitfire engine parts?"

"Well, we appear to have almost everything we need, apart from an airframe, but that's another story. No, what we are needing is a... is a Merlin 45 Supercharger. Might you have one of those?"

"A Mark Five, is it? The paper didn't say that. Let me think. Yes, yes, if I'm not mistaken, I think we might have a few pieces... will you let me call you back? Let me call you back... the shake of a lambs tail, Ted, I shan't be a minute."

"Of course." The line went dead as if slammed and I replaced the receiver.

Laura passed by.

"Mr Rutter?"

I nodded, my surprise palpable. But getting up to follow her, it rang again.

"Hello?"

"A Mark Five Supercharger, am I right?"

"Mr Rutter. Yes, that's it exactly, a Rolls Royce Mark Five Supercharger, for the Merlin 45."

"I can let you 'ave one for 'undred pounds."

"A hund..." He didn't let me finish.

"Alright, Seventy Pounds, not a penny less." He said, gruffly.

"Umm..."

"Are you wanting to take my arm off? What would you be willing to pay? Sixty Five..? Fifty? Forty?"

"Mr Rutter..." I interjected.

"Twenty Five pounds is my final offer, take it or leave it."

"I'll take it, Mr Rutter. Thank you."

"You drive 'ard bargain. Look, never mind all that. I'm not in the 'abit of asking favours, but would you do me the honour of doin' me a favour, Ted?"

"Yes, of course, if it's at all in my power to." I replied. This whole conversation had gone far faster than I was in the habit of, for something so momentous, but there was no dictating the pace with the man and I was reasonably pleased with Twenty Five Pounds for a working supercharger, if that was indeed what it proved to be. I might have thought twice if it had purely been for me, but as it was for Ash, I didn't hesitate. Indeed, he could have got a fair bit more, if he'd stopped sooner.

"Ted, I don't know the reasoning behind it, but she's got it into 'er 'ead that she doesn't want my 'elp, you understand? Now, I don't wish to stick my oar in where it in't wanted, but I can see you 'ave need of this supercharger and I would be pleased to see it go to 'good 'ome. Plus, I'm 'appy to 'elp my butterfly Bels, even if she doesn't know she's being 'elped."

"Yes, right." I said.

"So, what I'm asking for is that you say nothing of this 'ere business... that we keep it amongst ourselves, I would be grateful if you would do that for me, Ted, as a favour to me."

"Yes, of course, if that's what you wish, by all means. Certainly."

"I'm very indebted to you sir." He said. "Kids. They don't know what you do for them, do they, behind 'scenes?"

"That's very true." I said.

"So. I'll send Fred down with the van tomorrow, when I know of 'er movements and you can give the money to 'im. Cash is fine."

"Right, Mr Rutter." He really wasn't a man used to anyone saying no to him. That much was clear, but I had to say, I didn't dislike him.

"Am I right in thinking we understand each other, you can come up with where it came from, am I right in that, Ted?"

"Yes, I'm sure I can think of something."

"Champion. It'll be with you on the morrow, you 'ave my word on't."

"Thank you very much. You'll make a young man very happy."

"Right, well, goodbye to you." And with that, he put the phone down.

Sure enough, at Seven the following morning, Hamlet signalled the approach of an unfamiliar vehicle on the drive and, eventually, a polished Bedford van squeaked to a halt the yard. Gran took hold of Hamlet's collar as I went out to meet Fred; a slight, careworn man I recognised from the pub, very efficient and economical in his movements, I remembered him as a man rather partial to a flutter on the gee-gees, glued to the racing pages, pen forever at the ready behind his ear. He opened up the rear doors to display a bulky parcel, wrapped in ubiquitous oiled brown paper and secured with twine, as well as an additional cardboard box of oddments.

I had already accepted I was going to have to take it sight-unseen and work out afterwards whether I'd been diddled, but I strongly suspected this wouldn't prove the case. Between us, we deposited the parcel into a wheelbarrow and made for the workshop, Fred with the additional box of extra bits under his arm. It had been necessary to borrow most of Laura's housekeeping to make up the requisite Twenty Five Pounds, there being no time between phone call and the impending arrival to get to a bank.

I tried to give Fred another fiver for his troubles but he'd have none of it. He stayed long enough only to cast an eye over our prized possession, wishing me well in getting it finished and then he was off, no tea, no toast. Although I suspected some of the reason was he didn't much like the looks Hamlet was giving him through the kitchen window.

I contemplated our newest addition to the collection, deliberating whether or not to open it. I sorely wanted to, even if only to re-wrap it, but I had a feeling there was another pair of hands more deserving of the honour, so contented myself with a quick root through the box of extras.

It consisted a carefully considered collection of components that all worked off the supercharger, his reasoning presumably being that if the supercharger was missing or incapacitated, the satellite pieces no doubt were too and he was correct. Accordingly, a quick perusal offered up a Coolant Intake, a Twin Delivery Coolant Pump, various necessary piping-certainly a recognisable Throttle Heating Pipe for starters, Two Air Intakes, a Two-Speed Change Pump, a Twin Fuel Pump, assorted small gears, nuts, screws, and washers and, joy of joys, a brand new set of Magnetos. I had a feeling he'd done us proud.

I didn't ponder too long as to why Helen had neglected to include her father in her latent interest. Perhaps she had wanted to do something on her own, something even that might make her father proud, or perhaps she had a grudge against him. She was the right age for that to be a possibility and he was certainly abrasive and perhaps controlling enough to perceivably be a difficult man to live with, who knows. But the condition of all of the parts was nigh on immaculate. They looked like they were straight from the factory floor, never used, which boded well for the carefully parcelled supercharger.

I resisted the temptation to wake Ash and went back for the breakfast I had postponed with Fred's arrival.

"How is it?" Asked Laura.

"Well, I haven't unwrapped the main course, but the hors d'oeuvres look very appetising. Very appetising indeed." I said.

"Oh, good." She beamed.

Ash surfaced an hour later and I found him chomping toast under the unfaltering gaze of Hamlet, who actually appeared to look down at him when sat in a chair. Hamlet did love toast. Laura gave him half a loaf with his Pedigree Chum for breakfast, so he already knew he had a yen for homemade bread. He would cock his head, his mouth slightly open, drooling at the corners of his chops, eyes steady, unblinking on the toast in your hand and every move it made between plate and mouth, alert for any errant crumb, or the slightest indication that you were wavering in your intentions to eat all of it.

Quite how a dog straight out of the Styx, or something vampiric with Christopher Lee managed to resemble 'cute', I have no idea, but he really did his level best. Ash was pretty good at ignoring him. He knew no amount of toast would be enough, that it wouldn't even touch the sides on the way down and that he every day consumed a full loaf of his own, but the battle of wills was always engaging to watch.

"Good morning, Ash. When you're done here, why don't you come over to the workshop. I've a surprise."

"What is it?"

"It's a late Christmas present."

Throwing his crust to the dog, he finished his egg with suitably economic haste, scuttling upstairs to dress.

Shortly, I heard his hurried steps cross the yard and he came in, closing the door dutifully behind him, already alert for the new. His eyes soon lighted on the bulky parcel sitting squarely on the worktop.

"Is that it?" His eyes were huge.

"Yes."

"Is it for me?"

"Yes." I confirmed.

"Can I unwrap it? Who's it from?"

"It's from me and your Grandmother."

Forever bless him, before he even went over to it, he hugged me first, then approached the bench slowly, almost in trepidation, as if he knew what he thought it was, but was afraid that he was going to be disappointed. I suddenly feared that I might have got it wrong in not opening it first. What if he was indeed going to be disappointed? What if it was a crushed hulk of rust? A perfectly functioning supercharger for a completely different engine? I hadn't considered that and right now, I wanted for all the world not to disappoint the poor boy.

Examining it briefly from a couple of angles first, he then pulled at the twine tied in a tight bow at the top, which separated with a gratifying twang. He then slowly pulled the remnant string well clear before proceeding to unwrap the thick paper with great deliberation, as if defusing an IRA bomb. I confess I would have been far quicker in the execution if it had been me to reveal the prize beneath, but I rather delighted in this slow savouring of the process. It deserved it. And it was yet another reminder of how special it was to be a child. It was so lovely to be able to do something nice for him, something you just knew he was truly going to appreciate and in a way it got harder to do, as one got older.

I breathed again: the blower was indeed brand new. Somehow the man had bought and then preserved a 'charger, straight off the production line. It might even need running in. Extraordinary. I tried hard not to lean forward and look at it as if I had also never seen it before. But I could tell, just looking over Ash's hunched shoulder at the familiar profile it struck, that it was exactly what the doctor ordered; a Merlin 45 Supercharger. And this one worked. Of that, I had absolutely no doubt at all.

I sent a silent thank you to Mr Rutter and to Helen, who had obviously helped, even if it had been entirely unwittingly. I had a niggling worry that when Helen saw it, she might know where it had come from. It really depended on how familiar she was with her father's Spitfire artefacts. I could imagine she had already gone through it once her interest had been captured by Ash's quest. But we could cross that bridge when we came to it.

Ash leaned on the bench gazing at the Supercharger, not even touching it for fully five minutes, before he eventually turned around.

"Thank you Grandad. It's the best present I ever had."

"It's a pleasure, Ash. Thank your Grandmother too, won't you?"

"Yes, I will. Oh, Grandad is it going to work? Are we going to do it?"

I got up and approached the bench. I was still marvelling at the fact that anyone could have a shop-new MkV Supercharger even ten years on, let alone thirty. It was funny how things worked out, good and bad. But there really was no predicting it. That was what could sometimes be so lovely about life. Perhaps we'd both been in need of a bit of a boost. I smiled at my own unintentional joke.

"Well, I think we deserve a break, don't you? What say you get your overalls on and we give it a go?"

"Yes!" He didn't know what to do with himself, what to do first and I had to calm him down a fair bit before we could actually get down to seeing what we had. But it was apparent to me very quickly that it was all there and in excellent working order. I would love to have known how Rutter came by it, but I was even more impressed with how well he had looked after it in the intervening years. It was all too easy to buy something new, but let the grease harden, the oil evaporate, but this really was in perfect working order.

It then didn't take long at all to marry it up with the Merlin. The Supercharger looking at odds against an engine that had seen so much service, not to mention cremation and a burial. Ash was absolutely ecstatic. I had needed to do the heavy lifting, albeit with the help of a block and tackle and it was always a fag getting the two together, with the gears lining up correctly with the crank, etc., but there were then plenty of peripherals left for Ash to be getting on with on his own. Again, all of these were immaculate. My esteem for Mr Rutter peaked and I wondered quite how many other gems he must have under brown paper in his evidently impressive collection of spares.

"How do we test it? Can we fire it up? Should we take it down the field?"

Ah. Yes, I had forgotten to inform him of that little disappointment. But I had at least made some phone calls.

Chapter 19
2014

"Bridget? It's me. Hi. Look, he's had some sort of a relapse and they've taken him back into surgery. He's had a 'subarachnoid haemorrhage'. Sounds like something out of a bad B-Movie. What is that?" my attempt at brevity remaining just that.

She paused before replying, only the shortest of pauses, but long enough for it to mean serious. To top matters off, she then spoke in super-gentle and careful tones. Suddenly aware of the sound of my own breathing, I listened intently to what she had to say. I needed so much to understand.

"It's essentially a, ahh… ok, Ash, it's a blood vessel is bleeding in his brain. Now, they can treat this. They can coil the aneurysm…"

"What do you mean, what's 'coil the aneurysm' mean?" I said, pacing about.

"Ok, so you have bleeding in the brain. They can slip a thin piece of platinum wire into his femoral artery, in his groin… and guide it up all the way through his body. When it reaches the rupture, they just fill the hole with wire, blocking it off. And then maybe just help it to seal with some small electrical charges…"

"…No."

"It's a long procedure, maybe three hours." She added.

"He's going to die, isn't he?" I said, as if I had suddenly channelled a Medium, stating it as known fact. The air caught in my throat, under terrific pressure from my chest, preventing me saying anything further.

"No, not necessarily, no, no, he isn't. You can't think like that. He's in the best place, I mean, he's simply been wheeled from the ward straight in to surgery, right, so they've really caught it early. As early as they possibly could."

"Yes."

We remained on the phone together, neither speaking, only the odd crackle of the line signal that we were still connected.

"Do you need me to come down? I can come down."

I knew that was an imposition. She had a child of her own, a vocation as a doctor and a household to run. I wanted to say yes, but in all conscience, I couldn't.

"No, it's ok, you don't need to do that. Thanks. But if he's really going to be in there for three hours, there's really nothing that you can do here, seriously. I appreciate it, though. Thank you."

"Well, you just have to say..."

"I know. Thanks for being there. And explaining."

"No problem."

I heard some screaming in the background. It didn't sound terminal, but it was pitched enough to know that it more than likely required semi-immediate parental attention.

"You'd better go." I said.

"Ah. Yes. Sorry.'

"Thanks Bridge."

"That's ok."

"Bye."

"Bye."

I hung up and watched the screen of my phone as it belatedly indicated a severed connection and slowly lit out. I rubbed the unseemly transferred grease from my ear onto my trousers and pocketed my phone. 'Parental attention'. There was a phrase. I desperately squeezed my face with my hand as if in an attempt to rearrange the mask, then looked around, aware of my surroundings. No one seemed to have been paying me any attention. How many times had this scenario, or one like it played out in these halls, I wondered. I hated hospitals. Three hours. What to do?

St Mary's backed onto Paddington Basin, an offshoot of the Regents Canal. As I paced around the edge of the unnaturally still, murky looking water, for the first time in my life, I wished I smoked. Somehow it would have made perfect sense right then to fire up a Gauloises and smoke it hard to an incandescent nub, hopefully in just four long drags, then flick it to fizzle in the water.

I looked for something to distract me, not wishing to fall down a negative rabbit hole. A man on a bicycle going too fast in that cold, economical show-offy manner, but wearing a helmet. A woman on the phone walking with a nervous quickstep that indicated she wasn't that happy being in this shadowy no man's land and would be more relaxed when she reached the road on the other side of the tower blocks. Three young Asian men in suit jackets and ridiculously pointy Rumplestiltskin shoes swaggered past, each trying to outdo the other in their braggadocio. I realised that, only because I had brown skin, I was the chosen audience for their excess and pulled my head in even further to indicate total lack of interest. Just being outside sometimes, could seem too raw to bear.

There was an over-compensation going on with the next generation, refusing to be cowed with who the perceived enemy was now. Things were no longer as black and white as they at least seemed to be, looking back at the War. Now, we were feeling like the enemy. 9/11 and thus 7/7 changed everything, not only for those mothers, fathers, wives, husbands and children affected by the atrocities, but all over the country, where British-Asians felt under the microscope, felt the need to buy transparent backpacks. There was a period back there when no one would sit next to you on the tube, no longer 'because you had fleas', but because, by sitting one chair removed, they both communicated their sense of betrayed trust, but also that extra two feet would somehow reduce the impact of any bomb you might be concealing. So in the end, it was still black and white. Us and them. And the Darkies were, as ever, the untrustworthy ones that needed keeping at bay. It was such an untenable situation. To be suborned as a replacement child for the childless. Beaten into shape, but ever falling short, an object of suspicion and derision, there only to fulfil a clearly delineated function (one we had the unfortunate habit of growing out of), but nothing more, nothing thereafter. As if dogs should just be for Christmas.

Perhaps there was a valid argument that said that trans-racial adoption was a form of slavery: Slavery being a system by which people are treated as property, held against their will from the time of their capture or birth, refused the right to leave, or to demand compensation. After all, what baby willingly forsakes its birthmother? What child, for that matter? Certainly, they don't have any choice in it, they simply had to get used to it; like it or lump it, until they were so thoroughly trained; brainwashed, like the elephant chained to the tree for 10 years who, when released, continues to stand by the tree.

I smiled wryly to myself. It was an interesting, if inflammatory concept and one I could never imagine being brought up in parliament or any fine court of law in the land. My mother had been told my birthmother was too poor to look after me. A good enough reason perhaps on the face of it, to feel vindicated in relieving the poor Indian woman of her burden.

I had subsequently learned however, that single, pregnant women of colour in Britain had been given a heart-breaking choice, with hideous regularity. In the Sixties and Seventies, there were many white, middleclass families wanting children. The solution was to deny these vulnerable single 'Commonwealth' mothers any kind of Welfare support, if they chose to hold on to their child. However, if they elected to allow their new-born to be put up for adoption, they would be granted that support through their pregnancy. The kneejerk that had gone on with the current influx of Romanians and Belarusians had been there before, despite the figures reflecting the bonus that they brought to the economy on both occasions. Ironic also that many British-Asians were unhappy with the latest influx.

What kind of choice was that for an unsupported Black or Asian woman desperate and alone, in a foreign country that had *invited* her to be there in the first place? How would you begin to support, clothe and feed your baby, unable, unfit, or prevented from work? All that I had been through under that enforced separation... I couldn't begin to imagine how it must have been for those mothers. For mine.

Of course, to give her her due, my adoptive mother had no way of knowing that this was the situation for the birthmother of her new baby. She was only acting on supplied information. But then, looking down through even recent history, how often had that regrettably proved to be the case? The inherent sense of entitlement that this nation and by extension, its natives had in conceiving these circumstances was breath-taking in its arrogance, in its audacity and was moreover, something the vast majority of populaces of colour could never even comprehend, let alone feel. As my mind rolled these thoughts around, giving them inner voice and time, I realised how important it must be for America to be so concerned in their signal lack of education for the masses, under the guise of Education. For learning was a dangerous thing: it fostered ideas.

So. I had very successfully managed to avoid dropping down a rabbit hole then... I decided I would find a supermarket, buy a sandwich with as much mayonnaise as was humanly possible to cram between two slices of bread; I didn't care if it was with salad, prawns, or any kind of meat, vegetarian or not and then head back to the hospital. Even though I might still have hours to fill, I needed the proximity.

Besides, my mind was running at terminal velocity and the thoughts weren't good ones. None of them.

Chapter 20
1977

Home tuition consisted poetry. Lots of poetry, from Walter Scott, to John Clare, to T.S Elliot, Milton, Wordsworth, John Keats, William Butler Yeats, Gerard Manley Hopkins and all-sorts in between, but Grandad was at great pains to illustrate that they weren't simply abstract works, but could inform the way one chose to live life; that love could be a poem. I never fell across the ode I searched for though, of my cathedrals in the sky...

There was also Maths, Geology, Geography, English, Biology and a fair amount of Physics, but I no longer minded these subjects, no longer on alert for the inevitable race-based belittlement. If I expressed any interest in anything, the tuition expanded for a while in that direction. For instance, in History we were discussing the widespread use of slavery.

As a 12 year old, I had thought it was only the preserve of the Europeans on Sub-Saharan Africa, but it seemed that, over the centuries, it had been practiced by several nations across the whole planet, as spoils of war, for wives, workforce, or status symbols and practiced from Viking Scandinavia to Brazil, to India, to Australasia, Arabia to Rome, Portugal to the Americas, Holland to Mongolia, China to Hawaii, Ancient Greece to Britain, transcending the Ages of man and still very much in practice today.

But I was interested in how us Indians got to the Caribbean. Grandad didn't break his stride, but explained that after the emancipation of the slaves around 1840, the Dutch, the Portuguese and the

British had no one to run their sugar plantations. They indentured over a million Indians, lying to them, saying it was only a three-day journey and that they could return to see their families whenever they wished. They were then put on ships to Mauritius, Fiji and Trinidad, spending up to three months at sea, many dying en route. It was another slavery in all but name. But this was why to this day, there are such established Indian populations on these islands.

"How do you know all this?" I asked, not for the first time.

"I'm interested; I read." He said. "I must confess though, I didn't know the particularities of this Caribbean slave history until your mother adopted you, only then was I prompted to find out."

He taught me things I knew I wouldn't have learned in school, which served only to make me more interested. He informed me of my heritage in a way that made me proud. I felt I could ask anything at all and never be ridiculed. He would also have me learn verse, even speeches from Shakespeare off by heart that I would re-enact for Grandma on a Sunday, once back from church. He loved poetry.

Beyond this, he taught me concepts and ideas that no teenager should have any right knowing, things that I felt I understood as he said them, but struggled with straight after. Undaunted, he maintained that, in planting these seeds some might grow into comprehension, might spur action, eventually fostering wisdom and so he persisted... That 'with the Ego prevailing over youth, this thrusts that person forward to explore only with guile and cunning, with deceit; cloak and dagger. But, when the Ego has at last been put in its place, *alongside* 'feeling' and 'knowingness' and 'intuition' and all those things, only then can Thought begin to explore and unravel the Now with any sense of true meditation'.

That ''thought' always lags behind 'development' and that 'experience' is separate from 'thought'.' It was true, I didn't understand many of these things even as he said them, but I certainly went away and attempted to digest them from different angles, as I lay looking up at the sky from my tree, or the bedroom ceiling from my bed. I wrote it all down and studied the words deep into the night, but they mostly refused to sink into anything intelligible.

He was deeply concerned for the new generation. Their direct connection to the Wars being severed and what that meant for all of us, growing up. It was a worry he carried with him throughout his life.

Of the journey of aging being a shock to so many because, no longer a society of extended families, there was no one for the younger generation to learn from. So things like the iniquities and cruel surprises of dental bridges, say, or knee and hip disintegration and replacement, the inevitability of prostate cancer requiring a scalpel and nappies thereafter, all of these things became valid topics for discussion under the banner of 'Education'. A map, a familiarity to help negotiate what would, after all, happen to all of us, should we live long enough, was imperative if we were to diffuse its power to undo us.

So I was party to long, detailed descriptions of what it was to lie on a bed, fully sentient, with only one leg anaesthetised, watching the top half of a surgeon behind a half curtain as he brought a stainless steel hammer down on a chisel straight into the insensate bone of his knee and the resultant smell of his own flesh, of splintered femur.

Did I want to know these things? I would scrunch my face and wrinkle my nose, but I had a morbid fascination and found myself asking questions. It was only natural, as Grandad surmised, to know, to understand. Although there was a tacit agreement that these things would never be discussed in the presence of Grandma.

A Technology lesson might slip sideways into instructions on how to write a cheque and how they worked within the banking system. I would never have gained any of these insights from school, from my mother. Her conversations were like listening to chatter on the radio. Inconsequential things in the main, such as the ever-escalating cost of things and her love hate relationship with the cash machine. She became more and more quiet, which was even more irksome, as I realised the reason was that everything she dwelt upon had weighed in at the opposite end of the scale in terms of import.

With Grandad, things had become a dialogue that I could actively take part in, rather than a diatribe. He didn't treat me like an adult exactly, but as an equal. There was a respect evident that I had never experienced before and always room for a question.

Sometimes, looking at my grandparents, I wondered how they had ever produced such a violent woman as their daughter turned out. This said, I had no idea whether they were aware how she had treated me. She never hit out in company, merely warned with a look or a very quiet remark designed only for me to understand; that I was really going to cop it when I got home. It didn't seem right to go telling tales now.

Tuition was interrupted by a trip out to Folwell Aerodrome, covered by the 'papers as it was. There was quite a gathering at the moment of ignition, immortalised by a photographer, myself and Grandad standing in front of the test machine with our engine in it. We had, as Grandad suggested, concentrated on the Merlin and covered ourselves in glory, but I was already looking beyond. Even though the journalist spoke about the occasion being momentous, for me, it wasn't over, as it was nowhere near being a complete aircraft. What use was an engine on its own, with nothing for it to drive?

But if we weren't to be building a fuselage, then from where would we get one? And how could we afford to buy it, even if we did find one? Even with the extra coverage, no one came forward with a solution, other than a museum in Minnesota, keen on acquiring our Merlin for their collection, which I point blank refused. I couldn't work out whether Grandad would have taken the offer, as he left it entirely up to me, saying I had three days to mull it over.

I'd drifted around the farm, feeding the ducks, scratching my hello's to Pinky and Perky, worming the cats, powdering the chickens for ticks and fleas, but whichever angle I looked at it, there seemed to be no point at all, even though I was aware that I couldn't stick it in my bedroom and it was useless as a working engine without the requisite airframe to put it in.

Russ said 'sell it to the Yanks and buy a car with the money', but that was what he wanted to do. He'd been saving up for a new car for as long as I could remember. Helen was more sympathetic and could see that, having spent so much time on something, it was 'more than difficult' to let it go. It wasn't as if the museum was even going to use it as a working engine, but put it in a glass case for people to lean on. It didn't seem right, really.

So I came back with an unequivocal no, although I was a little afraid of how Grandad might receive it. He simply nodded and said he would let them know, so I was no wiser as to his own thoughts on it. In the back of my mind, I had a pie in the sky idea that somehow it might graduate one day to the Battle of Britain flight. I didn't quite know how I thought this was going to happen, as they patently already had their Spitfire, Lanc and Hurricane, all in perfect working order. We didn't even have a set of wings.

Eventually, I told Grandad that was what I was thinking. He didn't guffaw at the idea, but explained that actually the Battle of Britain flight didn't always simply use the same planes every time, but rotated several airworthy aircraft, as there was always a fair amount of ongoing maintenance that needed to be undertaken on the aircraft, which included some pretty comprehensive strip-downs that necessarily took the aircraft out of circulation for extended periods of time, often several months, as there weren't many places that could do the work and it was a long and painstaking process. Often, in the dismantling, problems would come to light that dated back to the war. There would be documented damage that had been fixed, but quite how it had been fixed often had the potential to surprise.

The following months were perhaps an inevitable anti-climax. I acquainted myself with yet more fleas, bugs and worms, to the annoyance of the animals concerned. Russ taught me how to snuff candles with an air rifle and I took my first open air poo. One thing I did teach Russ, although he never took it up, was kissing bumble bees. You waited for them to land on a flower and then leant in and kissed them whilst they searched for pollen. I never got stung, but he wasn't convinced enough to try it.

More home schooling. One highlight was the purchasing of a new twin-tub for Gran. It worked in concert with the mangle that sat above it. I enjoyed feeding the wet, soapy shirts into the rubber rollers and having it squeezed so hard it came out the other side a solid tongue of warm material, the water draining away down a reversible chute back into the tub.

That night I was in bed, reading a piece about the Guinea Pig Club; a bunch of airmen burned horribly in accidents who were hospitalised and used as experiments in the new business of skin grafting. They had a bond among themselves that no one else could penetrate, having gone through all they had gone through and facing the stigma of terrible deformity. They knew what it was to be different through no fault of their own. But the core drive to read exhaustively about pilots and flying had temporarily lost its shine and I put it down in favour of sleep.

As I turned my light out I heard an unfamiliar hum in the night air. I lay for a moment trying to place it, but couldn't. Unwilling to leave the warm nest I had created, I eventually got up and went over to the window. It was coming from the workshop and I could see the light was on. I struggled into my over-small dressing gown, simultaneously shovelling slippers on.

Slipping noiselessly downstairs, avoiding the creaky boards in case I disturbed Gran, I crept past a puzzled Hamlet, with a very stern but silent gesture at him to remain lying down and, above all, mute. You could never tell with him. Anything out of the ordinary and he would always see it as a potential new game involving him bouncing about wildly, whilst barking loudly. You only ever got him excited once. Which was sad really, for such a fun dog.

The kitchen door was still unlocked, adding weight to my theory that Grandad was still awake and up to something clandestine. It was odd being outside in the wind, the house dark behind me, with only the light from the workshop to encourage me. I walked quickly across the yard, careful to avoid the worst of the many duck deposits. Looking through the workshop window afforded me no extra information, other than that there was definitely some industry going on in there.

I deliberated what to do. It was cold and I didn't like being out. The moonlit clouds were going over very quickly and the farm felt altogether a different place at night. I half wished I'd brought Hamlet for company, but he would have been too much of a liability, even on his short leash. He tended to take you for a walk rather than the other way round. Without thinking too much more, I turned the familiar Bakelite handle and let myself in.

As I entered, I saw Grandad bent over the mill, lit up in full swing. As I approached, Grandad looked up but did no more, which seemed to signify it was ok to approach. I dutifully reached for my overalls and a pair of protective glasses before doing so, knowing better than to ignore the safety signs plastered all over the place.

I could see that what he had up on the mill table was an engine block. I looked at him quizzically. He glanced back and then took a moment. His expression very serious; troubled even.

"Sometimes there is red tape when there shouldn't be. When it actually stands in the way of safety, for example, as in this case. I discovered that the engine block was bordering porous, before we first put it together. Metal doesn't last forever, nothing does." He stopped for a moment and redirected the coolant on the cut as the tool made a pass along the block, throwing a fine aluminium swarf off the blade tip as it spun in a blur.

"There are very good reasons why people shouldn't be allowed to manufacture engine parts, as I said to you before. But in this one, individual case, I am taking exception to that rule. Our engine block is borderline unsafe and I am concerned that, with continued use, it would fail. Now, I know that because that is what I used to be paid to do; find accidents -ideally before they happen- and fix them. I also happened to be able to get hold of an unfinished block and have the knowhow to make a working one from it, although I have to say, it has been a long time since I did so." He smiled, one hand resting affectionately on the head of the mill, one foot up on a ledge, as he bent over the job at hand.

Chapter 21
  1977

The Spitfire was by no means unrecognisable. The airframe was all that remained in any complete state, like the carcass of a well-picked chicken after Sunday dinner, a delicate skeleton, wings, legs gone, barely recognisable in its current form. The rest of it was scattered in bits all over the large hangar, much of it painted a sickly lime green and either hanging from the ceiling on bits of wire, lying on a bench, or attached to massive, purpose-built rigs.

Unlike engines, there were no laws preventing the manufacture of airframe components, so it was possible to use the damaged piece as a template and manufacture new wherever required. That was not to say it was an easy job. No two pieces of a Spitfire were the same. Where the Germans had studied American production lines, Mitchell, the Spitfire designer had not. It was therefore a painstaking business replicating every wing rib, every spar. Some bolted, some riveted, some pressed out and others extruded.

Odd pieces leapt out as recognisable among the exploded debris. The pilot's seat lay looking a little discomfited on the floor, very small and not a little insubstantial out of its cockpit shell. Two fuel tanks lay stacked loosely, one on top of the other. Grandad introduced me to the airframe engineer, who walked us around the assemblage of pieces.

I had thought the engine hard, but this if anything, looked harder. There was so much more of it and it was all so big. He preferred to stick to the more recognisable pieces, showing me the machine guns, cannon and the instrumentation panel. I hadn't realised that it contained 'generic' instrumentation panel components, with the same oil pressure gauge as a Lysander, a Hurricane and any number of other aircraft, all bought from the same suppliers and painted in Radium for night flying.

He also outlined the problems they had had with the skin. Taking the original paint off had allowed many of the rivets to fall apart too, the heads sheared from their shafts. It took a very skilled riveter to replace them, especially with flat rivets, if they were to stay put and hold the skin firmly, without snapping off or splitting the aircraft skin in the application.

There was also an art to the making of the wing trailing edge. Any slight deviation therein changing the handling to a remarkable degree, so it needed to be put together with a great deal of patience and respect. Grandad was even more entranced than I was. It was evidently a whole new science to him too and he asked a great many deeply technical questions that soon went over my head.

I would often understand the start, such as the advantage of a Jablo (wooden) prop over a De Havilland (metal) one, being that it would readily shatter upon hitting the ground and thereby not destroy the crankcase, unlike a metal one, which would, but then the conversation went into the use and construction of highly compressed laminates and I would find myself tuning out, despite not wanting to.

So when they slowed to a stop I didn't, but continued on through the hangar, leaving them to it. As with our engine deconstruction, everything was religiously tagged with a number.

"So. You're the Indian with the Engine."

I turned to see a short, sweaty man with a shiny head grinning at me.

"Trinidadian."

"Quite fitting then that this plane is from India!"

"Mm."

"We watched your engine test with great interest. Very impressive. You must be happy. Your Grandad's a very clever man."

"Yes, he is." I said, grateful for something I could say with any degree of ease.

He moved ahead of me between the workshop benches, pulling me into his wake. Grandad was still engaged in discussion, so I had no real option. I assumed the man must be important, though.

"We got all the drawings from Hendon." He continued, waving his arms about like a ballerina. "Do you know what it is?"

"A MkVc, from the canopy and armament." I said.

He took a moment to peer at me a little harder.

"Very good. Very good, young man. It is indeed a MkVc. Originally an LF Vc to be precise."

He'd lost me at this point, I didn't know what 'LF' meant. But I smiled encouragingly. Ask a question.

"How far are you from having it all finished?" A shadow passed across his face and he looked down at his hands as they did a small dance on the bench.

"Ah, well, that's the question. That's a very good question. It all depends really on how they get on." He waved a vague hand again at the workshop, or the people in it, I wasn't sure which.

"We aren't far away though. Not far away at all. Basically it all needs to get put back together and the skin put back on. We've made all the pieces we needed to replicate. All the mending has been done as it were and let me tell you, it was pretty comprehensive. All the humidity out there, well, you'll know all about that won't you, probably good for you, but it's no good for a Spitfire, let me tell you. No good at all." He looked lost for a moment.

I thought it best to remain silent about my ignorance of the climate or indeed, humidity in India, never having been there. As with so many people, I couldn't understand why India, or me being Indian was all such a big deal for him. But I also knew that having a conversation with him about how Indian I *wasn't*, wasn't going to be helpful. Probably just make him more jumpy.

"So. Do you like our plane?"

"Yes, very much. What I can see of it... I should like to see it when it's put back together more."

"Of course, of course. So would I!" he said.

"What markings do you think you'll paint it?" I asked.

"My, you're a meticulous young lad, aren't you?"

I managed to smile again as I caught Grandad making his way across to us.

"He's been giving me the Third Degree." He said. Grandad rested his hand easily on my shoulder.

"He just wants to know his Merlin is going to a good home."

"Yes, well, of course. And that's very important, of course. Yes. Of course it is. We all want that. What do you make of it... they're doing a good job here, aren't they?" The last bit seemed more of a genuine question than a statement of fact.

"Yes, they are. You must be very proud. You've a good crew here.' Grandad nodded. 'I'm impressed with the work that's gone into it. It doesn't look easy, but then, it never did. That's why I stuck to engines..." He added.

"Ah, yes, the business-end. Talking of which, what do you think? Do we have a match made in heaven, hmm?"

"What do you think?" Said Grandad, looking down at me. "Do we have a match?"

"I was just saying I'd like to see it when it's all back together a bit more. And I asked him what he was going to do with the paint scheme."

Grandad smiled a small smile, but one I knew well and I was secretly very pleased that he was pleased as, in unison, we looked back at the funny man for an answer.

"Well, why don't I call you when we know a bit better the schedule of things in terms of the rebuild?" Grandad didn't answer immediately, begging more of an answer from Mr Uncomfortable.

"And... and since your boy seems to know so much about Spitfires, how about we let him choose what colour scheme *he* wants. How's that?"

They both looked at me and I looked at the floor for a moment to think.

"Yes, I'd like that. Thank you." I said. He exhaled.

"Right then. Let's do that. I'll give you a call and in the meantime, you can have a think about colour schemes." He did look awfully beaten up, as if I had somehow put him through Gran's wringer, although I wasn't entirely sure how I'd managed it. But it would be fantastic to choose the colour scheme.

As we headed back across the gravel to the car, Grandad chuckled.

"Well done, Ash, Well done you. Your Mum would be proud."

Helen was very keen to learn of the potential Spitfire body and wanted to be walked through everything that had happened and everything I had seen. She lay on the Den sofa, clutching a cushion in rapt attention, as I related all I could remember, finding the final part particularly funny. She had the most audacious cheekbones.

"Why don't you just come with us next time?"

"Can I? Oh, I don't know."

"Why not? Why wouldn't you?"

"I'll have to think about it. Will you let me think about it? And ask Ted if it would be alright."

"Of course it will be alright." I said.

"Have you chosen a colour scheme?"

"Well, yes, I think it would look good in a classic green and grey camouflage. What do you think?"

"So you're going to agree to it... to putting your Merlin into this airframe? Whose plane is it then, is it still yours?"

"It would be nice to see it in a working plane, I mean for the engine to be flying and all that. I think that would also make Grandad very happy. But I don't think there's to be any money."

"I suppose it would be great having the Merlin fly again. I don't know why, I just felt a bit resistant to it." She added.

"What do you mean? Why?" I hadn't seen that coming.

"I don't know. I suppose I always thought you would rebuild the original aeroplane. The one the engine belonged to. But that just isn't possible is it?"

"No. I know what you mean, though."

"Do you?" she smiled.

"Yes. But I'd rather this option than stick it in a museum, I like the idea it will fly again." I said. She sat up.

"And it might even get to fly in the Battle of Britain flight... you never know."

"Exactly. You never know. It's funny though. If you had asked me a year ago if I wanted to have something in a museum, I dunno, I would have loved that. To think I had something that was good enough to be there in a museum, with a plaque and everything. A year ago, I would have thought that would be just amazing. And everyone in my school going on a trip and filing past this exhibit and it would have my name on it. Not that they would ever give anyone a trip to America, but you know what I mean." I said.

"Will it be hard to let it go? When it actually has to go?"

"Yes. I think it will. We've spent so much time on it, haven't we? I really feel like it's ours. But I would rather see it fly again. I do think that."

"Yes, you're right. Well done you, though. Amazing, right?"

"Yes. It is." I agreed.

I looked at her. She looked so cute. She had a fluffy three-striped jumper on, white, baby blue and pink. It looked impossibly furry and warm.

"Who's going to fly it? Have you met the pilot yet?"

"No. I haven't even thought about that. I wasn't even sure I was doing it."

"And what is 'LF'... what did that mean, did you ask Grandad?"

"I looked it up. It means Low Flying. They modified the airframe, clipped the wings and made a smaller supercharger to make it faster and more manoeuvrable at low altitudes."

"Why?"

"So they had some Spitfires that were best at high altitudes, to fight the Messerschmitt's and some that were best lower down, for the bombers."

"Ah. Clever. It's amazing, isn't it?"

"It really is. There are so many variants. It was such an adaptable aeroplane. The only British plane to last the whole war." I added.

"They're very special, aren't they?" She kind of said this to herself more than me, as if more in her own thoughts than our conversation.

"They really are. I never realised." I always feared losing her attention. It was a constant worry that often made me overcompensate sometimes, whenever I did see her. I hated this default position I'd chosen, but I had no idea how to counter it. She meant too much to me.

The placing of our Merlin into its new body carried none of the excitement that the testing had. It was with a sense of sacrifice, of a wonderful chapter coming to a close, that I watched the immaculate MkV taxi across the grass, pause for a moment and then lean forward, as if dragged by a powerful, unseen hand, leaving the turf behind surprisingly quickly. Everybody was smiling and up, but I could sense Grandad beside me feeling something similar.

The thought of that was enough to bring a lump up to my throat for a few seconds, but I banned it from going any further. So that was that. I had done it. We had done it. I turned and looked at Helen, her attention fully caught up in the shiny bead now arcing up into the distance against the clouds.

"Thank you, Helen." This evidently surprised her.

"Thank-me… for what?"

"For everything. For all your help and buying things and taking me to places, you know, for everything, really."

"Oh, Ash. That's quite alright. Thank you… for giving me the opportunity. I would never in a thousand years have done anything like it if it wasn't for you." She gave me a hug, although not a full one. I was still feeling a little tearful and her hug brought it back up to the surface, even stronger than before. I wondered why it was that the need to blub always seemed to happen at the most embarrassing, inopportune moments. Like farts.

The Spitfire made a low pass, then waggled its wing tips and made a victory roll as it pulled skywards. Like a wave goodbye. It already didn't feel like part of me anymore. I suppressed the desire to lean up to Grandad and ask him if we could go. I knew it wasn't polite. I just felt so indescribably sad. Helen jumped and clapped as it made another pass. At least one of us was happy. I still didn't know who the pilot was, nor did I care.

The return to the farm cemented the sense of the anticlimactic. Grandad and I travelled back in silence, with only Helen animated at first, however she soon picked up on the pervading mood and sank into her own reverie in respect of ours.

The farm felt inexplicably emptier for the loss of our engine and, although Grandad never said a word about it, I could feel it was exactly the same for him. When it had been there it had given us both a sense of purpose, even if they had been slightly different ones. For him also a chance to revisit the past in some real sense, in a way I could only guess at.

Only Gran seemed to remain quietly consistent throughout, continuing with the daily routine of the farm as if nothing had changed. But rather like a tooth, the gap left in the workshop by the missing Merlin felt to be a great deal larger than it should. Headlined '*Not So Sadhu- Fakhir's Fighter Finally Flies!*' the papers ran the story with a dark picture of me standing under the prop.

Grandad compensated in some degree by teaching me the fundamentals of turning, milling and grinding. I was interested, an avid pupil, but yet it was as if the purpose behind it was now missing. I wanted to know these skills before, when I could have worked on the Merlin in earnest for myself. I also knew that, were I to trip over another in the courtyard tomorrow, I wouldn't have the slightest inclination to do anything with it. It was as if it had all evaporated with the passing of our original engine. I stopped reading Spitfire books and pulled the Airfix model down, the Blu-Tac leaving an oily stain on the ceiling. 'The Lord of the Rings' looked back at me.

Chapter 22
1977

One day, a posh envelope dropped through the letterbox. There had been a running dialogue with the Post Office for some time previously and they had only recently agreed to start delivering again. For two months Gran had needed to collect the post from the local branch, when the Postie had taken exception to a certain canine member of the family. Ordinarily, he would be indoors, but one day, he happened to be out of doors when the Postie arrived.

A man already well-acquainted with the bass-bark of the Baskerhound, he was always careful to get the post through the letterbox without carelessly thrusting his fingers in, as the Great Dane often lay in wait on the other side, barking excitedly at the phenomenon of 'post', as much as a trespasser approaching the door, then playing with it, but never actually coming in; surely irregular behaviour.

This one day in question, Hamlet had gone out to manure the pasture, something he liked to do well away from the house, where he could attend to business uninterrupted and with a measure of privacy. The Postie had with due caution approached, having never actually met the owner of a gruff bark he had dreamt about and, thinking the coast was clear as usual, had dropped the post through the door. But, as he had turned and started to walk away, radar off, attention drawn to the next batch he was going to need, Hamlet, ears ever alert to the unusual, must have heard the letterbox slam, as the Postie habitually snapped his fingers back from potential danger.

Head up, mid-poo, he arrested his evacuations and made post-haste to the courtyard from the bottom field in double-quick time; in time in fact, to see the retreating figure of the Postie, heading back up the mouth of the driveway.

Overjoyed with the fact that, having waited literally years, here was his first opportunity to confront the shrouded figure that had teased him almost every day in living memory. The man responsible for ninety per cent of the claw marks scribed frenetically down the back of a battered kitchen door and countless stern admonishments from a woman gravely disappointed with his lack of restraint or discipline, even under such provocation. He needed no further cue. Speeding up across the cinder yard, with a guttural growl emanating from his ancestors, he launched, smacking the hapless Postie square in the back, whiplashing him wide-eyed, legs akimbo through the air.

They landed together, Hamlet with pedigree precision atop the man's shoulder blades, where he remained, despite tearful whimpering struggles, as tyrannosaur teeth engaged in the necessary business of divesting the poor unfortunate of his happy-fat bag of letters. It didn't take long; strap snapped, stitching tore and letters were showered liberally about the yard, much to Hamlet's unbounded glee.

It was only when Hamlet engaged in destroying the bag in totality, holding it down with his forelegs and tearing it into tiny pieces with his incisors, that the poor man was finally able to pick himself up, his piteous cries summoning help from Helen, as he sought sanctuary behind a low apple tree.

There had then followed a series of (hand collected) letters between the Royal Mail and Gran, about the potential danger Hamlet presented toward any Royal Mail employees. It was eventually cleared up by the fact that the Postie had actually sustained no injuries whatsoever, let alone drawn blood, despite his arguments to the contrary (he did draw a fair amount of urine).

A Royal Mail official eventually came to visit and, with no little trepidation, met Hamlet, but ended up feeding him toast whilst Gran agreed to fund any replacement bag. It was also tacitly agreed that Hamlet be either restrained or indoors, whenever the Post was to be delivered. We were still finding errant letters for weeks afterwards that had been blown about the yard and lodged in the roses, the haybarn and even the duck pond. I found the remains of what might have been more than two letters in pieces no bigger than a ha'penny, behind the sofa in the Den, but allowed that to be our secret, disposing of them more thoroughly, on Hamlet's behalf.

What was funniest of all was the unquestioning family loyalty that the incident precipitated. Although nothing was ever made explicit, it was clear that all five of us, Russ and Helen included, found the whole episode hilarious, Helen most of all, having found the man, his face mired in tears and grit, trousers dark from peeing his pants and Hamlet having a right old time of it flinging the remnants of his bag around in a yard made Christmas with envelopes. Grandad said the Postie stopped going down the local pub when everybody started producing dummy letters and asking him if he'd lost anything.

The freshly delivered manila envelope was an invitation to see the newly restored Spitfire fly as part of the Battle of Britain flight at Duxford Airshow in the summer. It was felt that the extra press coverage garnered by the Indian Spitfire would be a good thing for the airshow in general. It was accepted that we would of course attend, however we might feel privately about it.

The big day arrived and everybody made the trip, apart from Hamlet, for whom the jet noises were deemed too loud. He wasn't happy about it and looked on crestfallen through the lounge window, as we departed up the driveway.

As we waited for the climax of the event, Sopwith Camel, Gladiator, Tri-plane, Lightning, wing walker and Harrier Jump-jet having gone through their paces, everybody's attention was drawn to the East. Sure enough, far in the distance, three indistinct blobs could be made out against the light of the blue sky. The unmistakeable throbbing hum of Rolls Royce Merlin engines heralding the arrival of the Holy Trinity: Lancaster, Hurricane and Spitfire.

This time, my heart did miss a beat. My excitement rose to a crescendo as the triumvirate swooped past in slow, grand majesty and I wished for all the world that I could be in that Spitfire, flying over the crowds over the airfield for myself. Wasn't that what this had all been about, after all? To fly and to fly in that legendary aeroplane. Grandad stood almost to attention as they passed, tears streaking silently down his cheeks, Gran clutching his hand in tight comfort.

One by one they landed and taxied off to the far side of the airfield and we went off in search of ice-creams to take the heat off the day. As we queued, Grandad's name was announced over the Tannoy, asking that he make his way to the Control Tower. He didn't look too surprised by this request, but motioned for all of us to follow. We duly negotiated our way through the throng and up to the barrier surrounding the Control Tower, where a Security Officer had a few words with him. Shortly after, he let us through and accompanied us to a minibus on the fringe of the airfield. We all piled in and were driven around the airfield to the far side, where two big hangars and a large assortment of aircraft lay scattered around, including the Lancaster, Hurricane and a familiar looking Spitfire.

Still unsure why we were there, we stood about appreciating a close up of the various aircraft that many of the patrons on the other side of the field would have given their eye teeth for. It was good that Hamlet hadn't come, because it would have meant Gran would have had to stay behind and she was as enthralled as the rest of us, looking at the standing history of aircraft gathered before us.

I turned to Grandad.

"Do you think it would be possible for me to go up in her?" I knew as I asked it what a futile, stupid question it was. Spitfires were single-seater aircraft, I more than anyone knew that. He smiled sadly at me.

"You and me both, Ash. You and me both."

I felt an arm around me and glanced up to see Helen.

"The pilot wanted to know if you wanted to go and sit in the cockpit."

I nodded enthusiastically. It hadn't even seemed an option even a few months ago, when I'd wanted less than nothing to do with the whole business, but now, here, looking at her on the apron, the sun bouncing off her nose, she looked fantastic and I felt proud.

"Great."

We walked over and got introduced to Pilot Officer Doug Renshaw, who wasted no time getting me up on the wing and into the cockpit, allowing Helen to follow up behind. As I settled in he caught my eye.

"I just wanted to thank you." He said.

"What for?"

"For this. No one else has done what you did. Remember that, Ash. No one else. And in doing it, you have brought so much pleasure to countless people. Look at them all, over there. Hundreds of people have made the trip here, from all over the country and the thing they were all waiting for is this. Your Spitfire."

I felt so embarrassed I literally squirmed in my seat, but he wasn't finished.

"What have I to thank you for? Well, firstly, on behalf of all of them, I thank you. But most of all, on behalf of me. You know, I never thought I would get the opportunity to fly one of these. There's quite a queue, believe me and quite a shortage of these." He slapped the cowling as Helen would a horse.

"Do you know, I became a pilot directly because of seeing a Spitfire when I was young. But I was all too late. They were decommissioned before I got my wings and try as I might, I was never in a position to get in one, although I came close a couple of times. I thought it was never going to happen. And then you dug a soggy lump out of a pond and I got to fly her. Thank you. From the bottom of my heart. Now. How can I be of service?"

He proceeded to walk me through start up procedure answering any and every question that either of us had for him. Helen tested the water, asking about flying vintage planes in general, explaining falteringly that her grandfather had flown Spitfires in the War, by way of validating her presence.

"There are different directions that one can go in-fighters, rotary engines and gliders, basically. All very different and flying them all, as I have now been privileged to do, gives a unique insight into the complete chronology of aircraft handling qualities, moving between the pre-First World War aircraft, through rotary engines, Kestrels, Merlins, of course-through to the jets of the Fifties."

After that, it was a free for all.

"When did bird strikes become an issue? I mean, those early planes weren't a concern for birds were they?" I asked.

"No, that's right. Bird strikes... 200 knots. A bird can get out of the way up to 120 knots, but faster than that, they don't have time. So it became an issue basically between the wars, as technology created faster aircraft."

"Have you ever had to deal with one?"

"Once. In a Hurricane. Quite a shock. It missed the prop but hit the wing. Left quite a dent."

"What was so special about the Spitfire beyond the Messerschmitt, they were pretty similar, right?" Ventured Helen, warming to the task.

"You had the confidence that you could pull to the limit in a Spit, because the stall speed was controllable. With that knowledge you didn't shy away from it, but pushed it for all it was worth. Other pilots in other aircraft didn't have that confidence in their aircraft, so didn't take it to the edge of the envelope in quite the same way. That gave you a tremendous advantage in a dogfight. Just knowing she wasn't going to flip out on you, so you could go right up to that edge, where you were going to black out and dip in and out of it. No other aircraft could do that in the same way at the time. Best cat in the Coliseum."

We chuckled convulsively at that one and I realised that, other than Grandad, this was one of the few times an adult had treated me as an equal, rather than just a child.

Eventually, everyone had a go in the driving seat, even Gran was persuaded to clamber up the wing, although they brought out a small set of steps to help. It was a great day.

Chapter 23

1941

My Shrew was beyond local repair and was going back to Castle Bromwich for a comprehensive strip down and rebuild. However, I was due to have a new Shrew for that very afternoon, two new Spits being flown in by women from the Air Transport Auxiliary: MkV's. The MkV was essentially a MkII airframe, but with a much more powerful engine in it. Rolls Royce had jammed a massive supercharger on the back of the twelve-cylinder Merlin, boosting the power from roughly 1200 to 1500 horsepower at 3000rpm, with resultant higher ceiling and speed. How they managed to do this and still wedge it in the same hole in the nose of the Shrew, I had no idea.

It was common knowledge among airmen at least, that there had been problems with the first few as they had been rolled out. With no real time to test this new Merlin 45 engine, frontline pilots had effectively also become test pilots, sometimes with terminal results. The new superchargers hadn't brought with them with any improvements to the oil cooling system, which meant that at height, the engines had overheated, bringing pilots back to ground, sharpish. Thereafter however, it hadn't taken the engineers much time at all to sort out this 'teething problem' and accordingly, the much improved Shrew was being rolled out just as fast as they could manufacture them.

That day, only two of us were briefed on the MkV, as only two of us were getting them. Myself because I had treated my previous lady so poorly and the Flight Lieutenant. Although it was also pointed out that I was one of the more experienced pilots (perhaps even over the hill at thirty five?). They were delayed however, arriving as dusk fell, so we adjourned 'til dawn the next day.

Without the cue to scramble and refreshed after a healthy full breakfast, which was unusual for me, I took my time to get to know my new Shrew. We had been instructed to take them up, play with them, do a few aerobatic turns... basically get acquainted. It was also important to set her up just as you liked, so that once scrambled, it was one less thing to worry about.

I strolled out feeling refreshed, yesterday morning's events far behind me. As I tripped down the steps, I mentally ran a checklist to ensure I wouldn't need to go back for anything; helmet, facemask, goggles, overalls, Sidcot suit, silk gloves, scarf, boots and parachute, slung over my back. No mistakes.

The instrumentation was almost exactly the same, it being a MkII airframe, but I knew she would fly very differently, not only with the engine improvements, but just because every Shrew did. Minute differences in the build meant that she would move through the air slightly differently from any other Shrew.

With my airmen at the ready, I pushed the fuel switch over to 'Reserve' and pumped the primer six times to flood the induction manifold with fuel, whilst Jack obligingly rotated the prop by hand. I flicked the magnetos on. These would provide the spark that kept the engine going once it was running, then hit the boost coil and the starter button in quick succession, providing a shower of sparks to my fuel whilst cranking the engine over, making it inevitable that she would spring into life. Sure enough, with a thick plume of smoke from the exhaust stubs, the new Merlin 45 roared, making the whole aircraft shake and vibrate, the noise almost deafening with the canopy still open.

The airmen withdrew the massive external battery used to help start the twelve cylinder engine and I waited the short while for the engine to heat up to 60°, my attention lighting on the radiator temp gauge. Thereafter, a great many things needed to happen in quick succession, if I was to get into the air without overheating.

I sat there, the hum and vibration of the engine passing through my body as much as the rest of the plane there was definitely an added whine to the engine noise I'd not heard before, watching the temperature rise steadily. One of the chaps that failed to return was the one I had taught. Vincent. We had marked his passing with an ale. A raucous, sober ale. I pushed the oxygen open a tad and, as soon as the temperature hit, checked the two magnetos each in turn, switching them off and on one by one. The Shrew would certainly get you home on one alone, albeit at reduced performance.

Satisfied thus far, I pushed the power up to zero boost, checked that the propeller worked in terms of 'Coarse' and 'Fine' settings then, crucially, that the magnetos still worked at high power. I was looking for a reduction of around 150revs per minute with only the one working, so flicked them both off and on again in turn, waiting the few seconds required for the revs to settle and give me a true reading. Throttling back to idle and waiting once more to content myself that the engine wasn't going to die on me now I'd reduced the power, it was time to get her off the ground as quickly as possible.

I double-checked the prop was set to 'Fine' for maximum revs at take-off. The hot weather not helping matters, the radiator temperature had rocketed to almost 80° in just the short time it had taken to do basic checks. With chocks away and a quick exchange with the tower, I zigzagged my way onto the grass airstrip, temperature ramping. Cleared for take-off and with the temp now just over 100°, I wasted no time. She needed a lot of air pushing past the radiator and crawling overland with the landing gear also baffling the air intake meant for hot and bothered.

The airframe and instrumentation may have been exactly the same, but even when she was initially fired up, it was immediately apparent that this was a very different proposition from my old MkII. Sure enough, take off was noticeably quicker, as I ruddered to counter the prop rotation, she climbed with astonishing speed. Landing gear up and canopy finally closed, she champed at the bit to go faster and I was in no mood to stop her. At 150mph, I pushed the prop over to 'Coarse', feeling it correspondingly bite more air and the whine change, dropping rpm, but gaining speed by the second.

The clouds stood magnificent in the morning sun, the tall cumulus creating huge buttresses in the air. Flying close, at the right angle, with the sun behind, not only did the prop light as bronze as Hercules shield, but you were treated to the most spectacular rainbows. Not just ordinary semi-circular arches, but complete, iridescent halos that gradually shrank down as you flew towards them. Your own personal rainbow no one else would ever see.

There was something about this and about the extraordinary, gigantic, overhanging arches created by these clouds that somehow conspired to bring one back to earth, but to the high vaulted ceilings of the greater cathedrals. As a fascinated tourist, I had been fortunate enough to visit Lincoln but also Norwich and Westminster, however, none of these could compare to the majesty, the grandeur up here, the sunlight playing upon the constantly rolling, evolving clouds, shining gold, white, oranges and pinks, stretching ten thousand feet up into the air, embodying some sort of forbidding, impossibly ephemeral solidity, framing against the endless, deepening blue. If there was a God, then this was his playground, these enormous columns the pillars to his temple. I looped the loop, pulling Gee, timed to roll through those wonderful arches, rejoicing like a Junior Pilot in her enhanced capabilities, accelerating upwards.

Her optimum combat level, full throttle height was around 18,000ft, but we shot through that, the glorious map of England unfurling beneath me, such that I didn't actually register altitude again until I was well over Angels 35. I felt light-headed, energised. The very definition of alive as I spiralled heavenwards, my souped up Shrew purring like a dream, invincible, even as my vision tunnelled, blanking grey and I lost all consciousness.

I surfaced to a scream. I had no idea where I was and couldn't decipher what I was looking at. What and where was that dreadful noise coming from? Was I screaming? I tried to touch my mouth. Then disparate things began to coalesce, one after the other, by degrees. I was sitting... I was boxed. Pinned. I was looking through heavy glass... at... at Kent. Coming up to meet me. Should I be screaming? I was in a cockpit. I had knowledge of this. Indeed, I was in the cockpit of a plane I was flying.

There seemed to be an urgency to the current situation with which I was resolutely failing to grapple. I grasped the stick in front of me that wasn't there before, more by force of habit than any conscious decision- as my eyes rolled across their orbit with impossible slowness, to familiar but nonsensical spinning dials, the altimeter plunging in reverse, as I continued to process the evidence, gaining a sharp litany of insights into my current situation. If I could just...

What a perfect, blithering idiot. I had passed out, yes and through my own peerless stupidity, my earlier lyrical euphoria nothing more than the drunkenness of hypoxia, a lack of oxygen to the brain. Belatedly, stupidly, I cranked the gas open even, as I plunged to earth; all I had needed to do was increase the oxygen flow as I ascended above 10,000ft but, unused as I was to the improved ceiling, lost in the beauty, the speed of it all, that was the one key thing I, the Pilot's Instructor, had neglected to do, mesmerised by the newfound agility and power of my Shrew. Anger shot like a tracer through my recovering brain, instantaneously bolting through my limbs as I heaved back sharply on the stick; my second mistake.

Attempting to come out of a dive something in excess of 600mph, the airframe simply wouldn't cope with the forces I then loaded upon it. The First Law of flying any Shrew was that you adhere strictly to Her rules; you don't start applying your own. Something snapped. Cracked. There was an almighty bang and then air rushing everywhere, as if someone had left the kitchen door ajar and the wind had caught it.

I recollected bein' on me farder's fishin' skiff as a very young chil'. He would only take me out on the calmest of days. These were the days I looked forward to the most, when we walked the short distance down to de beach, clambering aboard just as dawn appeared, the sea sparklin' beautiful.

The air was so fresh, air that had never been breathed coming across the water lappin' on golden sand. I would crouch on de side an' look over the edge into the cool, dark-green crystal waters, sometimes clear through to the rocks far below, my eyes scannin' de shadows for de shoals of fish silver-sidin' in the sun. Barracuda. Turtle. Octopus. Shark. Specially on the look out for rays shiftin' in de sand banks, which Pa would stick wid a spear, quick as lightnin', bare feet glued to de bleach' wood, sometime followin' the harpoon into de water to mek sure he hit it right.

And when he haul' in de lobster pot, I would catch sight of it arcin' up out of de darkness long before dem break the surface and when he had emptied dem of their precious cargo and stacked them in the prow of the boat, I would then get to my favourite part. I would study dem carefully an' pick off de minute, baby crabs hiding in dem knot of the pot an' rope, among de barnacles an' seaweeds that serve to disguise dem pots on de sea floor an' I would rescue them, I would save them and drop them over the side, back into the water.

Perfect, miniature, working models of real crabs, that's how they appeared to be, but models that nevertheless needed the utmost respect and most delicate handling. The size of a thumbnail, they were so light, they would barely break the surface and then they would sink oh, so slowly, down, down, down, claws akimbo. Some with legs scrabbling sideways to swim back down, anything to hasten their descent downwards to the hidden, secret sanctuary of the depths.

But others would just float, would drift down as if in slow motion, suspended animation. And I would watch them slip-slide from view, as their mud-green carapaces merged indiscernible with the penumbra of inky blackness eagerly reaching up to meet them, drawing them back to its welcoming bosom.

At dawn after a full moon, at that most Holy moment of change, a space opens up between two worlds; the real and the celestial, this world and the spiritual and a drop of nectar fell from the heavens.

Chapter 24

2014

After the funeral, I decided to take a detour with the ashes. Returning to the farm felt hard, but somehow very necessary, reinforcing yet comforting the sense of elemental 'bereftment' I was feeling. The entrance to the driveway had changed a little, the drive smaller, the trees larger.

The biggest changes really applied to the yard though. There were no geese, no Hamlet bouncing out on springs, no horse to shake a dismissive mane. Not even trace of the pigpen; the fence had gone and the ground no longer churned up with hay, their red slide no longer in nettles against the fence.

Taking the oldest key of the bunch, I opened the workshop door. Everything had gone, but for a shrouded presence in the middle of the acute emptiness, the monolithic mill, hunched in silent repose. The top was wrapped in sheet plastic, tied with cord, but the green base remained exposed. My eye fell on a spot where the paint had rubbed away, the iron smooth and shiny, polished by the constant application of a rubberised safety boot.

What to do with it? How did one sell such an object and still imbue in the buyer the import of the item, beyond the superficiality of it being an out-dated, underpowered machine-tool with baggy bearings? How did one sell it at all? I understood the shrines that loved ones built to their dead, adorned with earrings, bracelets and hair-locks. I understood too the proliferation of house clearance companies, willing to step in and desecrate where emotion cut the bereft off at the knees.

My shrine only needed that one centrepiece; an ancient, green milling machine, well past its sell by date, sporting a bald foot-patch. I rested my palm on one of the wheels. How would I sell it for scrap? Did refusing money from those same people make it any easier to get rid? Any better?

Bea had prevented me from going to their funerals; I was more at fault for letting her, I saw that. It was my one true regret, neglecting to honour either of them. Looking back, I still couldn't comprehend how I had allowed her to. How I let her create more drama that kept me away. It was as if, even in death, they weren't allowed to have anything of me, any quarter of my feelings, my love, my time, but it was inexplicable how I had let her. I was worn down, but it was no excuse.

It was the ultimate act of jealousy, of ownership and control on her part. I didn't know how anyone could even want that, let alone act upon it, but I remained even more bemused by my ongoing acceptance of her dictum. What was I thinking? What spell was I under for that ever to make sense?

During Gran's illness, Grandad had scaled the farm right back, bit by bit, shedding responsibilities one by one, as he found it harder to cope with the day to day, planning for the inevitable. Russ had moved to Australia, fallen in love and married a Greek Cypriot.

Surveying the vacancy now surrounding me, I couldn't conceive of the wrench, as Grandad sifted through and got rid of all of his beloved engine parts, the larger machine tools and all the bric-a-brac associated with a lifetime's attention to detail. It was so admirable that he had still done it, no doubt with one eye on the fact that if he didn't, then I would have to. Both of them were so fastidious in their own way; so considerate, aware of the size of their own footprint and their impact on others, good and bad.

I found myself walking down to the bottom field. The hen house was still there although empty, the fencing all but absent. As I passed, I suspected a fox might even have taken up residence in it, judging by the fur-lined entrance. Perhaps the smell was too good to resist, or else he hoped in vain for some returnees.

The pond was noticeably more overgrown, the bulrushes having made significant inroads into the middle, making it impossible to throw even flowers onto the water, let alone ashes. Turning back up to the bridleway, the last thing to do was sit in my tree. It was harder to climb and much higher than I remembered and it felt more than a little vertiginous when I finally scrambled inelegantly up to my perch. I was unfit. So many memories. I had experienced so much, sorted through so many things sitting in this very spot. The bark still retained a worn shine in the seat.

Where had all the time gone? What did I have to show for it? What would I have done differently? At that moment I realised, for all of her faults, my mother knew that by putting me with my grandparents, she was doing a great thing for me and I looked upwards, silently thanking her for that wisdom and sacrifice. Something undoubtedly unhealthy had gotten her to adopt me in the first place, but she had come good in the end, albeit in the most crazy, unforeseen way.

The dissipating vapour trail of a distant, silent jet scarred the sky above and I twisted and craned to catch sight of the aircraft itself, ploughing its furrow in the sky.

For many years I had thought it must be Grandad that had first planted the seed of fascination I had with planes but, although he had no doubt fed and watered that enthrallment and over many years, I now recalled different.

When I was young, running to hide from my mother's ire, be it after a beating, or moments before, I would often find myself hiding behind curtains, on my bedroom ledge, or out in the garden. Very often I would look up from my refuge and see distant, mute aircraft flying over, so high that the sound of their passing wouldn't make it all the way down to me.

I would gaze longingly at those clean, sealed capsules glinting in the sun, their white trails streaming so gracefully behind them and I would wish with all my might that I could be inside one, travelling far, far away to some distant land, not a care in the world; a dream-like, flawless, escapist solution to all the pressing problems in my life, the perfect mix of the tantalising and the impossible.

The great, Unanswered Family Mystery I woke up to far too late was why, having committed his entire life to aeroplanes and flying, why Grandad had never once flown himself. Not even for a holiday. He'd built countless engines, poured every iota of himself across endless reams of flight data, had even sat in aeroplane cockpits with the face of a child on Christmas Day waking to find a lumpily-stuffed stocking at the foot of his bed and yet he had never climbed into an aircraft of any description, either as a pilot or passenger and lifted off the ground. I found it unfathomable. But in the end, even though our love of aeroplanes, of the magic of flight stemmed from such divergent sources, yet it was enough. It was enough to bring us together and it was enough.

The last I knew of Helen, she had taken herself off to Argentina and found work on a ranch and then become a jockey. In hindsight, I understood she must have been very much in love with Russ. To this day, I had no idea why he wouldn't have been any less than thrilled, but who was I to preach wisdom in affairs of the heart? Her father had eventually flown out and brought her back.

She'd attended university, but studying what, or even where, I'd no idea. It had been all too easy to let go of the thread between us and now I regretted losing both Helen and Russ. They were family, present at what was possibly the most important chapter of my life, if I excluded Tom's birth. I looked down at the urn and gave it a pointless embrace.

"What to do with you now?"

As with pain, it would seem we have no memory for the extremity of grief. Perhaps this select amnesia is the soul's antidote to certain insanity, even if the stain should remain indelible. The chaotic shock that swamps the void left behind engulfs, invades all before it like the fabled tsunami, having first emptied the beach of water. It has no distance, only creates it.

It becomes the onus of others to carry the afflicted through the ensuing days, the necessary arrangements and the funeral beyond, when it is all one can do to sleep, to breathe, to dress, to eat, failing to glaze the eyes to the immediate, innumerable reminders that surround every turn in the house you once shared with your living, laughing being. Bridget was my dutiful angel.

It was all I could do not to keep his service a secret. To keep it entirely to myself; some bizarre sense of covetousness demanding that no one else should be in attendance, that only I could mark his passing. If they wanted their own service of remembrance, they were welcome to it, but for me, there was no celebration of his life to be undertaken. His life was celebrated daily, moment on moment by his living, not his passing. Sanctuary from his school friends ably ensured by the hard insulation of a deep whisky tumbler, peering blearily out through cut glass and a smog of peat fumes, when all of my anger, all of my hate was for myself.

There was something about the Lord's Prayer that seemed to revert grown, sentient adults to children as they bowed their heads and recited it; the years would roll back. Any critical faculty brought to bear on the rest of their lives was stripped away, as the cant lines were trotted out with an unquestioning innocence, it was all I could do not to rail against it, even as they spake it. It was like some spell. As if the words were so powerful, so elemental, they were above either analysis, or dissent.

The box of his coffin oxymoron, the embodiment of everything and absolutely nothing at all, his death the antithesis of sense, devoid of meaning. Someone once said that we were all essentially on our own, that we all die alone. I had felt as a twosome with my Mum, until she passed, then a three (even a four) with my Grandparents, briefly a one again and then a two, soon to become a three with my wife and child and I even with all of it, was content enough.

But she had died in bizarre fashion, a pointed question mark, like an unattached brass hook, hanging forever over the void she left behind, leaving me with a young boy, so ill-equipped to know what to do and how to cope. But then, you just did. At least we were two. Now, I reflected, as I sat up a tree like Winnie the Pooh with a pregnant pot, rather as Helen had held me the last time I had lost someone, I was again, one.

All that effort. All that time, all that investment and all I had to show for it was a sturdy plastic bag and an urn, full with the ashes of my child. It was a complete waste of time even considering the question 'why?' or even 'why me?' How many people through the Ages had come to this point for themselves, through war, or some myriad dreadful misfortune? I understood why Ancient Greek women beat their breasts, rent their clothes and pleaded piteously to oblivious planets, for only they understood at cellular level what it meant. And yet, I didn't want to *do* any of that.

I shoved a hand into my pocket and it closed around the familiar palm-sized slim box of matches. For now, I decided, I just wanted to make my way home as invisibly as I could, not speak to anyone, not catch anyone's eye, without touching the ground, nor even disturbing the air as I passed, that I would be left alone. Front door rattle, take off my coat, kick off my shoes, perhaps placing the urn, that vase with my flower in it on the hearth, whilst I considered what to do with it. I negotiated my way out of the tree, almost coming a cropper at the last bit, staggering with my own weight as I jumped, landing heavily, the urn under one arm. Refusing to look any more at the farm, I headed back to the car and set off up the driveway.

How much of these ashes were my son? How much the leftovers of the person going through the oven before? How thorough were they with clearing up? How much the wood of the coffin itself? What percentages, I wondered. I was aware that my thought lines, my normal processes had completely splintered. I would seem to flick from one disembodied thought to the next without even the need for censorship, or any kind of coherent join. I didn't care. I just needed now to close the door. Be at home alone, on my own. Curl up in bed and pull my quilt over my head. Just for a while.

Going upstairs, I slowed past his bedroom door, wondering whether I was going to open it or not. No. Not this time. I rested my fingertips on the stripped pine. It would still be there when I was ready. Right then, I understood my dilemma quite calmly: Whether or not I loved him more than life itself. If I did, at least the solution was clear, if not the method. I just needed time to think it through, carefully and calmly.

I awoke to the phone ringing and, against my better judgement, picked up whilst consciously clearing my throat, aware it might be Bridget, who'd left strict instructions that I was to answer all her calls. It was an automated message selling something I didn't hang around for, beyond 'Please, don't hang up…' The house was quiet, patiently awaiting my next move. Through thick Edwardian wall, a baby's muffled yell drew breath to push harder on the second volley. How would it be if the mother never arrived to quiet the terror in its soul? Turning over, I pulled the quilt up round my shoulders, one ear at least stifled to its cries.

The phone rang again and I paused for two rings, wondering whether I could bear to let it go through six before the machine took it. Realising I couldn't, I lifted and dropped it. However, it rang again almost immediately. I picked up and held it to my ear.

"Hello. Is that Tom Wycherley?"

I hauled myself up and attempted normal.

"No, it's not, why, who's calling, sorry?"

"Well, this is Dan at FS. Is he there?"

"No, I'm afraid not. Can I ask what this is concerning? What is FS?"

"Folwell Services."

"Folwell."

"Yes, we restore vintage aircraft."

"Oh, yes, I see. I know Folwell..."

"Is he your son?"

"Yes. Yes, he is."

"Ah, ok, that makes sense. You see, we had this call from a guy, left a message on the recorder, only he sounded quite young, so we got to wondering whether it was a hoax." He said. "Then we got a call from a Bridget someone. I didn't join the two up at first…"

"What did his message say?"

"He asked that we call this number and, ahh... Well, he was wanting to sort something out, left a long message and got cut off before his time, if you get my drift." He chuckled.

"Sort something out…?"

"Yes, but... I think it's best I speak to him, though. When's best to call back?"

"Dan." I closed my eyes. "It is Dan, isn't it?"

"Yes, that's right."

"Dan. My son passed away. He was in an accident and..." Well, that was it really.

There was a breath and a short pause down the other end. I imagined him holding his face with his free hand and awaited the apologetic retreat.

"Mr Wycherley.. I'm… so sorry. I'm so very sorry for your loss. One moment. Just give me a second, will you? Please, don't hang up."

I listened to Dan as he covered the mouthpiece securely, the earpiece giving that odd creaking noise as his palm moved over the microphone whilst he spoke at length to someone else presumably present his end and waited. The infinitely patient, ready, motionlessness of a harvest spider caught my eye, slung in alert tranquillity, like a harpist awaiting the drop of the conductor's baton, upside-down and all-but invisible under the coving. Presently, the hand came off the microphone and he returned, in quite unexpectedly business-like tones.

"Mr Wycherley. Do you have a pen?"

"Yes."

"Can you come to Folwell on Sunday the 18th?"

My eyes slid automatically to the bedside calendar.

"Yes."

"That's great, Mr Wycherley. '10am ok? I'm correct in thinking you're familiar with us?"

"Yes. 10am. Right."

"We'll see you then, then." He sounded oddly cheery, definitely smiling as he said it.

"Yes, right. Thanks."

"My sincerest condolences, Mister Wycherley."

"Thanks. Bye." Still completely nonplussed as to exactly what I was thanking him for. Had I just been hoodwinked with some elaborate ruse?

"Goodbye, sir."

I hung up, leaning heavily on the phone for a moment as I stretched awkwardly out of the bed. My son's will, reaching from beyond the oven was, on balance, one inarguable reason to remain breathing for another twelve days. The Eighteenth was also my birthday. The poor facsimile of Tom's face grinned back at me cryptically from the Order of Service on my bedside table.

Next to it, an acrid-sweet new box of Swan Vestas matches and a small scrap of yellow foolscap I'd always intended to copy into print, so preserving its words. It didn't take me long to realise I didn't need to though, as the words etched their power more permanently, written as they were by my Grandfather and only discovered by me when going through his papers.

Friendships
'Friendships, like headlamps lavish distant darkening hillside,
Shining so merrily, brightening their way as they sweep along,
Only to dip out one by one,
Some abrupt,
Others fading into waiting solitude;
Recumbent weight of mountain black
Ever harder to discern
Against cloaking skies.'

And then-

Laura
'As harbour dinghy, moored

Fickle moon may beach or float

The Four Winds will blow

Tides do ebb and flow

Sailors... come and go

But, whether you will or no

I'm always bound to your shores'

Certainly, he lived his life with a concentration, an economy and a belief: as close to an ode as anyone I knew.

Chapter 25
  2014

Folwell was very different. It had grown a fair amount since I was last there, clearly signposted from the motorway as it was and now offering a prominent Visitors Centre to greet ones arrival, adjacent to the gravelled car park. Early, I sauntered over, one of the first there. To the left was a large, functional cafeteria gearing up for the day and to the right a gift shop stuffed to the gunnels, selling everything from bomber jackets to fridge magnets.

I walked around slowly, taking in the panoply of books now available that hadn't been around when I was a child. How I would have loved this shop, with its posters, its Air Ministry Spitfire Handbooks, repro uniforms and RAF key fobs.

The first time I had come here was with Grandad when I was 13. The Merlin was complete, but we'd remained unable to test it. I had always pictured that we would mount it on some sort of rig in the bottom field and fire her up, a great roar from the twelve well-appointed cylinders drawing a smile from Russ, scattering the geese and giving it back to the cockerel. But it was far more complicated than that. Controls and gauges needed to be attached. Any tailor made rig would need to be incredibly heavy and stable. We also required a fuel tank and it all needed to be made safe.

No, the easiest and most comprehensive method for testing an engine was actually to drop it into a functioning aircraft, well-anchored to the floor, tail up, to bring the plane horizontal and then you had all the bells and whistles you needed already attached, rev counter, temp gauge, fuel, throttle lever, etc., so you could really put her through her paces, adequately monitored. It was four months before we found a potential surrogate, a visiting aircraft in for servicing at Folwell that would then to have her own engine reinstalled.

That Monday, a short mauve low-loader arrived at the farm, the Merlin was manhandled on, bolted to the original angle-iron stable rig, then securely strapped down. All of a sudden I remember feeling panicky and possessive, not wanting the lorry driver to leave with my Merlin. We followed up a day later, to find the final checks to the engine-install taking place, on a brisk but bright morning, outside No. 2 Hangar, Folwell. Merlin engines were designed to go in and out incredibly quickly, which of course made sense during a War.

In the days before the Health and Safety Act, 1974 had really caught on, my Grandad leaned down and advised I pushed the two protruding spurs at the front of my earholes in, adjusting them as necessary, if it got too loud. I was more nervous that the engine would just explode and all our work be for nothing, but after an Age of pilot pre-flight checks and a general thumbs up all round, he at last fired up the motor. The prop spun a couple of jerky rotations and then, with a splendid plume of smoke from the exhaust ports, she burst back into life. A phoenix from the lake, to mix metaphors.

I remember it being a momentous occasion, I was so happy. I never felt more affection and gratitude for my Grandad than I felt then. He was a remarkable person and I, a fortunate boy. The most generous, patient and clever man I had the good fortune to know; a guardian angel in greasy overalls, when I needed one most.

We jumped in unison and clapped when she finally roared once more, 36 years after she had plummeted so ignominiously from the skies, smuggled silent by water, entombed in clay. It seemed such a long time since I first shuffled uncertainly across the crack-baked crust of Baggett's Pond, edging towards the middle, almost afraid that the earth might give way; that I would plunge into an unknown underground lake, my drowning cries never to be heard. What followed proved to be, if anything, something of a symbiotic rescue.

If I remember rightly, Helen wasn't there, only the inaugural flight. It's funny not remembering that. She meant so very much to me, back then. Those that we have loved and lost; friendships that at the time meant everything. Of their place and time, they remained everything. Looking at the middle-aged mum regarding me from behind the till, I shook my head at the ingénue I was. I wish I was able now to take the hand of that boy, to kneel down and tell him a few things. Despite his suspicion, he was only ever able to see the best in people and believe what they told him as the truth. A great quality to have, many might say, but one so fraught with danger.

Moving out from under the curiosity of the shopkeeper, I passed through to the canteen and got myself a coffee and croissant, sitting so I could look out across the somewhat melancholy airfield, even though nothing discernable was happening.

I got together with Beatrice in 1997 through mutual friends, at a New Year's Eve party. On Putney Bridge, at two minutes to midnight on December 31st,

1999, the year both my grandparents passed away, with a nervy, desperate peak of adrenalin, I went down on one knee asking for her hand and we held each other tight, as the firework display to end all firework displays bombed its way up the Thames. I was in love. In late 2000 we married and, two years later, we had Tom.

In retrospect, even when I had just met her, I could feel something was wrong, in that she failed to connect in any real way with the intimacy I needed. She made no room, no time for it. But back then, we were living at opposite ends of the country, so it was easy to shelve, in the belief that when we finally got together, it would all get sorted out.

When we did finally get together, the disparity was even more evident, but we both had the pressures of work and it became easy to allow that to be in the way. If we could just... if we could only... there was always a target, some nebulous time in the future that I believed -if we could only reach it- things would completely transform and we would then be able to make the time for 'us'. I carried on moving forward with even more determination to 'make it work'.

All the way to the end, I had a totally misplaced belief that I could change her. It was my own ego more than anything, underpinning a shamed incredulity that I might have got something this critical so drastically wrong. An illness. So, as I began to grapple with the magnitude of the problem, it became about fixing the problem and that then seemed to entail fixing her. I made it my job as a man to be bigger than the situation I found myself in; to be patient, resilient, endlessly kind and forgiving. Surely these were honourable qualities to possess.

After six years together and a young child however, I understood that it wasn't just me. She was the same with our child. There was an awkwardness, a fundamental lack of engagement that spilled over into that mother/child bond. The union I thought so precious and perfect, so fundamental to nature, of which I had been robbed- she didn't have it.

And nothing I could do was right, however hard I tried. After Tom was born, there was no more sex. At all. I finally managed to get her into Couples Therapy, with a lovely woman I quite fancied, if I was honest. I thought I felt the therapist begin to come over to my side, as she began to understand the dynamic between us, but for a while it became all about managing Bea's neuroses. About what I needed to do to help her, so of course, I did it in spades.

But it was wearing; I had for a long time begun to look forward to the gaps when I could escape, alone with Tom, with work, or even just a night off and I would drink to numb the senses and turn down her volume in my head. She treated me with disdain. She could even ignore me entirely; come home after a day's work and not even bother with hello and I in turn would tiptoe around her 'appeasing the Goddess', as my therapist was fond of calling it. After a three year abstinence, there followed an abrupt 180° turn, when Bea decided she did in fact like and indeed, need sex. So we had sex all the time, to the point where I became terrified I wasn't going to be able to keep up with her insatiable demand. Then she decided that although she needed sex, I was no longer the person she wanted it from, so we should 'take a serious look at having an open relationship'.

Of course, through all of this, I thought about leaving my Princess Madonna. From one day to the next, I wouldn't know whom I was going to come home to. I developed a molten ball of lava that rolled around in the hollow of my gut, yet still I remained strong, not allowing all that she threw at me to outwardly affect me. Of course, it did. I realised in hindsight that I had become taciturn at work and also a bit of a bully. It was tolerated, as I also happened to be a boss, but it changed the dynamic at work and at least three fine, talented, upstanding individuals left as a direct result of my actions.

But still I felt that I could change her, kidded myself that every swing in her behaviour was progress. No sex to a surfeit being the main one, at least for a while. But I wasn't strong enough, or man enough, or even psychoanalyst enough to fix her. My skills, I learned, lay in very different spheres, ones to do with empathy and kindness and sensitivity: for the love of my son. And this was my undoing, because she knew I would never do anything to hurt him. She could play around with my sensitivities, abuse me, ignore me, taunt or oppress me, safe in the knowledge that if I left, she would get the boy and moreover, that I would never put him through the trauma of that separation anyway. It was an uneven playing field and she wasn't 'playing' anyway.

I was over a barrel, with no conceivable way out of the situation I found myself in, because if I left her, not only would she take the boy but, in my own mind at least, I would be seen to have failed. Failed as a man, but also to have deserted her and her son in their time of greatest need. For she was extraordinary at charming and beguiling others into believing she was some put-upon angel. For those that worked with her, she was a tireless, amazing, sensitive, fair, well-adjusted paragon; a 'real' woman of strength, endurance and determination and a mother to boot. Most of our friends were her friends first.

If I was going to walk away from that, I really would be leaving everything and there wouldn't be one person that knew us who wouldn't instantly side with her. We both knew I wouldn't be able to face that. My ego wouldn't take it. And so I stayed, stayed to let her throw her first extramarital conquest in my face with 'a man who was more of a man than I could ever be.'

Miserable and often drunk, I hunted for friendly waifs or strays, anyone that might find a father with marital problems enough of a proposition to take to bed with them. The only time it did happen, I still wasn't man enough to actually go through with it. Even though she was a hundred miles away, Bea still pulled my strings. I was down and I knew it; pinned-, ground-, emotionally-, you name it. I drank a little too much, flirted a little too freely and was stoic and strong in all the wrong places.

But yet I had my son. She had given me that one gift beyond jewels, beyond land, or notions of ownership, beyond any palpable thing. The time I spent with him was the most precious, demanding, beautiful, amazing, fantastic, forensic, desperate, freefalling, delicate, powerful treasure. And she could see that, see what it did in me, see the bond that I had with him, look on helpless at the laugh I could elicit as bath-times took him to Mesopotamia on a Hippopotamus and she truly hated it. She was jealous for the one thing that she knew she could never have and I realised that she would do all she could to break that chord between us. Either that, or she would break me, using that cord to do so.

In the very week when I girded my loins, scraping the spilt playing cards of my life up off the floor, understanding clearly that whatever I tried, I was never ever going to understand her, she didn't want to be understood and that whatever I tried to do it could never ever be right; that there would be no 'justice', no payback for all of my patience, my sacrifice, that she would never 'catch up' with me and comprehend the error of her ways, love and gratitude springing from her eyes.

In that very week, when I understood properly that I had managed to marry my mother, when I had decided that, come what may, I had to go and that this was the greatest decision, not only for me, but for our boy. I would take away with me the tension in the home and he would still see that even though I wouldn't be there to kiss him to bed every night, he would know when he did see me, that I still loved him more than ever and that this would never dim. In that very week, she died.

I've heard that it's remarkably common for people to do drastic things on losing a parent, perhaps by getting married quickly, or having a child. For me, it was losing my grandparents, but the result was the same. I got married very quickly thereafter. Needing to make something work, to get on with 'life' and do those stock, meaningful things with it, like marry and have children, without really being able to clearly make out the reasoning behind, the motivation for these actions, but also disabling my natural selection process, my own system of alarms that might have prevented me making such a dreadful mistake.

Do people consciously see that vulnerability to take advantage of it, is it all subliminally executed, or else pattern of behaviour; the jigsaw of captor and willing captive merely selecting itself as a 'best fit'? What is the final advantage for them, if what they do is built upon deceit, they must know that at some point it might all come apart at the seams, leaving nothing but dereliction in its wake.

I knew of very few good young marriages. A few from the older generation, but so many of my friends were in various states of unhappiness at their partner's behaviour and seemingly unable to negotiate a way out of their own personal hell, with the kids held too often as sole reason to remain together.

Looking back as we all inevitably do, I knew in my heart I was making that mistake, but smothered it. I felt now that I had paid the price for that particular act of asphyxiation. And, when I was left so unexpectedly with Tom, after the initial shock and no little guilt at the all-pervading sense of total relief, of dark prayers being answered, it just became, well... great.

I had Tom and a huge weight had been lifted from my shoulders. Gulliver's pins had been raked from my prostrate frame. The whole anticipated jig I was going to have to negotiate around my ex-partner no longer existed and all the energy I had previously expended on that bottomless, aching well, I could now focus completely on my boy.

Of course, everybody rallied around, me being the blameless, grieving, newly widowed single father. I did love her. I was bonded to her and might never have truly managed to cut the ties I felt to her; the need for her approval, for her love burned so thoroughly, so deeply within me. I guess I would never know whether I really, truly could have done it on my own.

I was robbed of that knowledge the moment she gunned down the fast lane of the A33, only to hurdle the central reservation into an oncoming artic. The lorry driver was traumatised enough to give up trucking altogether but was, at least physically, unharmed. He needed to retain contact with me for some time thereafter, through a strong sense of responsibility and guilt about which he made no bones. I however, felt no animosity at all toward him, which after a while he finally accepted. He made it clear though that Tom should want for nothing in the future and if I ever had need of assistance, I only had to ask.

We'll never know why she did it. Why she turned left at speed, where no left turn existed. The Police investigation only deepened the mystery. She hadn't been on the phone. The car was in perfect working order with no discernible mechanical failure. Witnesses testified to the fact that nothing untoward had happened to make her swerve, there was nothing trying to cross the road, nor any vehicle acting erratically in the vicinity.

Her prized Range Rover had bounced up over the curb, launching off an overgrown mound of earth, almost cleared both crash barriers, landing at an angle in the opposing fast lane, one rear wheel caught by the barrier on the other side of the road. There was a definite argument pointing to the fact that if she had been in a less well-appointed car, it couldn't have mounted the barrier in the first place, merely plough into it, having smacked the curb then grounding on the bump first. But she had always had a thing about being 'classy', with Range Rovers falling into that bracket. Personally, I could think of few things less classy than the word itself.

All in all, seven other vehicles were involved in the incident, but thankfully with no other major injuries. Her death had been as instantaneous as it was inexplicable. I couldn't for a moment believe that she was at all suicidal. Or that, even if she were, she would be able to commit suicide in such a complicated and extreme fashion, putting other's lives at risk, let alone time her twist of the steering wheel to coincide so perfectly with the topography of the roadside at that precise point. A split second either side and she would merely have impacted with the barrier rather than ramping over it, presumably saving her life a she slid to a halt, the ample car crumple zones taking the brunt of the impact. She had her safety belt on. Statistically, women preferred pills anyway.

It was Jung who said of all of the thousands of clients he'd seen, or even heard about, what actually happens to them and the way their lives turn out was always a surprise, not only to him, but to the client themselves and no one, however learned or intelligent, could have come up with the answer that they eventually lived out.

When I turned Thirty, I made the first faltering steps to seek out my birth mother. I'm not sure why it took me so long to do so and I did so with the blessing of my grandparents, with whom I remained close, until Bea, when everything positive pretty much stopped. It is said that to have another language is to have another soul. I would say the same for those adopted, whether they have another language or no, but those two souls can drift forever broken, consigned to sifting for jigsaw pieces that will never quite fit. Tracing proved a long and draining process and one I failed to complete.

It was the thing I most admired about my Gran and Grandad. They seemed to fit. They had absolutely no need for anyone else. Perhaps they fitted too well. It would explain my mother's violence, which seemed to stem from a deep frustration, an insecurity emanating from of her mistrust of men and a predilection to see everything as a competition for love and affection, rather than a belief that there was always enough to go around.

Both her mother and father loved her, but with a measured calm I had witnessed for myself, borne of total inner security, that perhaps didn't suit her growing up and that she also didn't appear to have inherited. I guessed, deep down, she knew she could never compete for the love her father had for her mother. That must have been very hard. It would have taken a maturity one simply wouldn't have had as a child, even as a young adult.

Of course, I sidestepped all of this. So often, skipping a generation can transform the potential of a relationship, once the grandparent is relinquished of the responsibility that a parent has. It was also compounded in my case by my being both adopted and being orphaned at such a young age.

My grandparents had been consummate guardians. Perfect role models. As I sat here nursing my cup, I reflected it was just a shame that I had chosen my mother as my relationship role model, rather than my grandparents. How young these patterns are inked into our souls. These dark bone fibres introduced to their greenstick threads. How deep the dynamite laid.

One of the many legacies of adoption, a gift and a curse placed side by side in a cracked pot if you like, was the manifestation of hyper-vigilance. The curse of hyper-vigilance is you seldom forget. You *see* everything and you never forget vast tracts of your past. The details of your childhood that nobody else, if asked, can ever recall even if they try, are etched into your brain like circuit boards in acid. Part of the ongoing compensation your seared brain undergoes with the trauma of losing the one thing, the one being that made any sense, that made you whole. Your entire being then goes into overdrive, concerned above all that through no further carelessness of your own will you ever go through such a cataclysmic error again, such is the loss.

The gift of course, is that you remember everything. Observe and absorb the world around you with a totality, needing to grasp and understand all that you can, in case it be needed for survival at some point in the future. Thus human dynamics become your bread and butter.

On his deathbed, my grandfather explained to me, in his own quiet, inimitable style, that there were five main regrets raised by people at the end of their lives:

1) Wishing they had the courage to live life true to themselves and not the life others expected of them. 2) Wishing they hadn't worked so hard. 3) Wishing they'd had the courage to express their feelings. 4) Wishing they'd stayed in touch with their friends. 5)

Wishing they'd let themselves be happier.

He concluded that, all things being equal, he wasn't guilty of any of them. And that he hoped that this could in turn be an example to me. It was most unlike him to talk out of turn, to be erring at all on the side of arrogance, but I could tell, as he gripped my hand firmly with his, that it was overridingly important I understood what he was saying. At this point, hand on heart, could I say the same? My respect and love for this man was absolute.

When Gran was diagnosed with dementia, he cared for her until the end. For the final two years, he even had to lock her in the house to prevent her running out and getting lost, or causing injury to herself or others, by wandering into traffic. Even when she no longer knew his name, fought him tooth and nail, kicking, punching him, wiping her arse on the towel and pissing in the corner, he never quit.

He bore it all with a patience, perfectly safe in the knowledge that, if it had all been the other way around and he had lost his marbles, she would have done exactly the same for him.

Even as his life horizons were shrinking, the enormity of the territory being revealed to him for this, the last part of his journey, grew vaster by the day, swallowing not just planets, but whole solar systems. The courage needed to deal with his final chapter built upon all he knew, all he had learned in the decades leading up to this point, deciding for him what he clung to and what he let go; where if anywhere, the fear lay and so how peaceably he accepted the thickening.

When she finally went, to my own private relief more than anything, an unrecognisable, tortured scrap of her former self, it was as if he realised he could finally let go; that his work was at last at an end. The concern lifted from his face, like years falling away, Atlas put down his rock and took brief respite, then he passed peacefully, sleeping the sleep of the Righteous, just two months after she had. His final words to me, in his inimitable dry sense of humour, were 'Be any age. Be a hundred, but stay young. Don't ever get old.' This last sentence was said with such knowing, such compassion, almost as a kind of rueful warning, that they brought tears to my eyes, even before I realised they were to be the last I would hear him utter.

He was cremated, true to his wish, without a Christian service, his ashes mixed with hers and scattered at Westcliffe-on-Sea, the place they had first met and spent many an hour, paddling, laughing together in the shallows, trousers and skirts pulled up to their knees, cockles in vinegar.

In these modern times, if ever an example of what it meant to be a man was needed, I never looked any further than Ted. There was a quietness to true courage, to fortitude, that remained at odds with the current whirlwind of that which the media considered important. I had so wanted to be a good role model for Tom. I felt I had so many things waiting in the wings for him, to reveal when he was old enough. It was so exciting just thinking of the things I would be able to share, that I could allow him to discover. Where was all of that now?

"Mr Wycherley?" I twisted round, surprised to be recognised as, usually, no one expected an evidently Indian looking man to have such an English moniker.

"Dan. Dan Farrow. Thanks for coming. Let's go through, shall we?"

Walking back through the shop, we ignored a No Entry chain and proceeded down a corridor.

"I took the liberty of Googling you."

"Ah." I said.

"You were the boy with the Spitfire."

"Yes, guilty as charged." I said.

We went through a hangar with a couple of ancient, delicate looking biplanes, presumably predating even the First World War and into a second, smaller hangar, more a workshop than an exhibition hangar, I observed.

"Do you want to see if you can get into these?" He held up some overalls and a jacket, eyeing me for size as he did so. I didn't see any point in arguing, after all Tom wanted me here and I had managed to do that.

We walked on, Dan passing me a well-used, soft leather flying helmet and goggles as we did so. We exited the building and headed out across the concrete toward the Control Tower. Skirting that, we passed between a couple more low buildings on the edge of the airfield.

It was a grey, unremarkable day to be flying. I wondered what aircraft we could possibly be going up in. The Tiger Moth was built for two. With this get-up, I doubted it could be something modern. We passed between some large 1950's passenger aircraft, a P40 and a couple of trainers I couldn't immediately name, when Dan stopped abruptly and took hold of my shoulders, preventing me from moving.

"Are you ready for this?" he said. I nodded, despite having no idea what I was agreeing to.

"This… well, this is the present your son wanted you to have." He turned me through 90 degrees and I stood blinking at a Spitfire. But it wasn't an ordinary Spitfire; it had been modified, a second Perspex hump interrupting the familiar, sweet lines, in profile. It was a two-seater.

"Happy Birthday."

Steering me firmly by the shoulder he led the way, aware I was in shock, gracious enough not to expect anything coherent in response. He showed me where safely to place my feet and helped me hoist myself un-athletically into the passenger cockpit. As I settled, my nostrils filling with the very particular mix of leather, fuel, oil and rubber, I automatically tugging at my helmet to make it comfortable and adjusted my goggles, under Dan's concerned scrutiny.

"Your pilot for the day is Flutter." He said as he leant over, strapping me securely into my seat and fitting the oxygen mask, ensuring it was also switched on. It took me a moment to register he meant the pilot's name. I thought it odd somehow not to meet him beforehand.

"One more thing, I almost forgot. Tom had a message for you. It didn't make… well, the message was that he 'found your poem'." I nodded.

"He found your poem." He said again, making sure I'd got it, even if he hadn't.

I was in complete and utter shock with the speed of everything. Dan patted my shoulder then closed the canopy, stuck his thumb up and then disappeared from view.

Shortly, the Merlin spluttered then burst into life, as I sat pinned in stunned wonder, channelling Rudy

Maharaj, the whole aircraft vibrating through the seat of my pants as much as my ribcage and all of the organs in between, the rank taste of rubberised air taking some getting used to, as much as the overwhelming sense of restriction, securely trussed up as I was.

After a few minutes, we zigzagging forward, taxiing across the runway and turning back to a halt on the grass, as the radio crackled into life, the female pilot enquiring in clear, flattened tones and Control giving permission for take-off. The engine accordingly wound up in pitch and we rolled bumpily across the grass, quickly gathering momentum, the hangars and stationary aircraft whizzing past the right-hand wing like the flickering pages of a book. The tail had already lifted and, softly, we were airborne and turning.

The land beneath us was overcast and shortly we hit a low ceiling of cloud, everything blanking grey as we continued to climb, water streaking the Perspex, finally bursting through what must have been a relatively thin blanket of cloud, out into the bright, unexpected sunlight above. Out into the cloudscape of my long lost poem.

"Happy Birthday, Ash."

I knew that voice.

Vaulting ever skywards, turning, humming, the sun catching the prop and the wing as we arced up at last towards the clear, beckoning clouds of my childhood, seemingly soon to be within touching distance for the first time only now, cathedrals in the sky indeed, rising up with all the vasty expanse, all the resolve, the power, of an idea.

"Helen."

Flutter. Of course. Helen 'Flutter' Rutter. Some jokes are years in the making.

A never-ending vapour-scape, stretching all the way to the white, palest blue of the horizon lay in every direction, finally lifting through seamless hues to the strongest of blues, on the edge of our envelope, directly above.

Helen, the Spitfire, now propelling me through space and time, the overarching clouds more eloquent than any foggy lines from school: A slate quarry, ten thousand-foot cliff faces of darkening purple giving way to rolling, regimented hillside fields of cushioned lavender. Steep anvils on a massive scale, the playground of the Gods, upon which impossibly large bronze swords and shields were hammered with lightning bolts, thrust back into the furnace of the sun and quenched in the oceans.

Cotton wool tundra as far as the eye could see, fields sprouting pink, yellow, white candyfloss trees, smooth lakes with tiny islands, grey forests giving way to more sinister-seeming, ageless, dark-grey shadows, hiding secrets through the Ages in their folds. Grecian faces, gold and white against the blue. Glimpses of a distant land, far, far below.

With a starburst sense of coming full circle in too many ways at once, grinning through a prism of tears, I took my deepest breath: He found my poem. All of them.

TALE FIN

Bibliography

First Light
                    Geoffrey Wellum
Spitfire A Test Pilot's Story
                    Jeffrey Quill
Spitfire Owners Workshop Manual
                    Alfred Price, Paul Blackah
The Spitfire Story
                    Alfred Price
The Hardest Day
                    Alfred Price
The Spitfire Story
                    Peter R March
Spitfire Ace
        Martin Davison, James Taylor
Nine Lives
                    Ron C Deere
Duel Of Eagles
                    Peter Townsend
Shot Down In Flames
                    Geoffrey Page
A Nation Alone
                    Arthur Ward
Spitfire Manual 1940
                    Air Ministry
The Spitfire Pocket Manual '39-'45
                    Air Ministry
Pilot's Notes - Spitfire VA, VB, VC
                    Air Ministry

If you enjoyed this, you may be interested in the next book by Andrew Rajan, another character led piece, but this time a high-speed romp through the darker world of poker...

The Big Game

Small-time London player 'Shanks' is looking for the biggest poker game on the planet. As far as he's concerned, everyone's on the make. Everyone is trying to take lumps out of you. It's eat, or be eaten.

But if he can make enough money for Vegas and get there for the World Series Main Event, maybe, just maybe, he can earn the right to show what he's made of; sit down with the big boys in the Big Game. Getting arrested wasn't part of the plan.

www.andrewrajan.com